Reconciliation, Healing, and Restoration of the Church

Finding the Mind of Christ
"So That the World Might Believe"

by

Patrick Joseph Hession

Copyright © 2011   Patrick J. Hession

All rights reserved

No part of this book may be reproduced, stored in a retrieval system, or transmitted by any means, electronic, mechanical, photocopying, recording, or otherwise, without the written permission of the author.

ISBN: 978-0-6152-0265-5

Cover photo by Penny Hession

All Scripture quotations are taken from the New American Bible, copyright 1970 by the Confraternity of Christian Doctrine, Washington, D.C., including the Revised New Testament, copyright 1986.

Other books by the author

Wordseeds from the Wilderness: Calling God's People to Reconciliation, Healing, and Restoration
God Is Your Family: The Key to Your True Identity and Self-Worth
God Is Your Family: Reflections in Scripture EPub
Intimate Prayer
Life's Net
Preparing the Army of God: A Basic Training Manual for Spiritual Warfare
Christian Homebuilding for Men
Christian Homebuilding for Women
Men – Planning for Marriage
Women – Planning for Marriage

All we have is God!

Where charity and love prevail,
There God is ever found.
Brought here together by Christ's love,
By love are we thus bound.

With grateful joy and holy fear,
His charity we learn.
Let us with heart and mind and soul
Now love him in return.

Forget we now each other's faults,
As we our faults confess,
And let us love each other well
In Christian holiness.

Let strife among us be unknown,
Let all contention cease.
Be his the glory that we seek,
Be ours his holy peace.

Let us recall that in our midst
Dwells God's begotten Son.
As members of his Body joined,
We are in him made one.

Nor race nor creed can love exclude
If honored by God's Name.
Our brotherhood embraces all
Whose Father is the same.

-*Ubi Caritas et Amor*
A Medieval Hymn

Table of Contents

About This Book	1
Honoring the Truth Teller	5
Pastoral Leadership for Which the Lord Is Looking	16
The Gentle Force of the Servant	27
Servant Leadership Is an *Attitude* and an *Asset*	34
Toward Reconciliation, Healing, and Restoration of the Church	37
Jesus Christ's Vision and Order for his Church – Part I	69
Jesus Christ's Vision and Order	72

for his Church – Part II	
The Church That Jesus Established	76
The Source of Truth and Unity in the Church - Part I	90
The Source of Truth and Unity in the Church - Part II	106
The Source of Truth and Unity in the Church - Part III	131
Ministries and Offices in the First Century Church	153
Gifted Ministers	159
Apostles in the Church	163
Apostles in the Church – Further Reflections	166
Prophets in the Church	179
Baptism – A Command and a Gift	184
The Eucharist: Sacrament of Unity or Symbol of Division?	200
The Mother of Jesus in the Scripture and in the Church	226

The Ministering Body of Christ: A Call to Action	237
Church Teaching on the Sanctity of Life	247
Be Careful How You Sow	262
Bibliography	267
About the Author	269

About This Book

On the night before he died, Jesus prayed that we would be one, as he and his Father are one, so that the world might believe in him. As his followers, we are either working with him to achieve this unity so that his prayer would be answered, or we are hindering his work of love and unity.

For too many centuries now, leaders in the Church, and in faith communities, sects, and denominations, seem to have been more interested in propagating and furthering their own theologies and agendas than in building up the Church in love. Fundamentalism, Evangelicalism, and Pentecostalism are not denominations to be triumphed but aspects of the one Church. Jesus gave only one commandment that reflects his agenda: Love God with your whole mind, heart, and strength and then love others as you love yourself. There is no other agenda. This is the work of the Church, and this is the work of each of us as members of his Church. Laws, doctrines, and practices must help us achieve this purpose or they must be discarded or changed.

If you have been more interested in building your own kingdom than in building the kingdom that Jesus came to establish, it is time to repent and to change. You are either building unity in Christ or you are sowing further discord and division. Change of direction means change of heart and attitude.

The purpose of this book is to prepare for the latter. It is a collection of articles and other information that attempts to focus on issues that have divided the Church for too long so that we can begin the process of working toward that unity for which Jesus prayed. It can no longer be a matter of who is right and who is wrong. We must get back to the mind of Jesus and what he had in mind when he established his Church to continue his work "so that the world might believe."

The only way to do this is the way of humility, of giving up positions, doctrines, and fears that keep us apart from one another. Pride of position must give way to the lowliness of servants who hear the Master's voice and follow it, regardless of the cost. Jesus is not an -ism or a denomination but a

Person who all Christians agree was sent by the Father to bring us into his family through the Spirit. Over 45,000 "churches," sects, and denominations can no longer proclaim that they are "the way, the truth, and the life!" We must all find our way back to the mind and heart of Jesus!

We must start listening to what the Spirit has been and is saying to others in his family who are listening. We must start speaking to one another and discerning whether what we believe and teach is really what Jesus taught us through the Spirit. We may need to accept the fact that what we thought was the voice of the Spirit in times past was really the voice of man and is no longer valid for the work of Christ. There is only one voice and one Spirit who was sent to bring to our minds all that Jesus said. We must choose to come into obedience to that voice and to seek out others who are also listening to that voice, whether they are of our faith persuasion or not.

Many have been doing this in the Church, and much progress is being made toward reconciliation, healing, and restoration of the Church. My prayer is that this book might be one small contribution toward that effort. The information enclosed has been culled from many sources, both non-Catholic and Catholic. Sources are credited when possible and can be found in the bibliography at the end of the book.

Honoring the Truth Teller

Values Produce Predictable Behavior

Prior to 1993, I was an active duty Army Chaplain. During that season in my life, I taught leadership skills to officers and non-commissioned officers in leadership retreats as a part of my ministry. I often used management games to teach these leaders about leadership.

In one management game called "Powerplay," a scenario was created where these leaders were arbitrarily divided into groups by virtue of winning in a trading scenario. The winning group was then given authority over the other groups. The winning group had the right to make the rules for future trading and to dictate these rules to the other groups. Without exception, the group with authority always began to make rules to keep its authority and to benefit it in trading. Given enough time, the winning group began to clearly abuse the other groups. This group justified its behavior on the basis of winning in the earlier portion of the game and by virtue of having the authority.

Reactions of Different Abused Groups

In those retreats where non-commissioned officers (sergeants) were involved, the sergeants would allow themselves to be taken advantage of. Their overriding value was loyalty to the authority, no matter what transpired or how unfairly they were treated. They were unhappy and grumbled among themselves during the abuse but did not productively oppose it. They offered no feedback, no confrontation, and no truthful interaction with the abusive group of sergeants. This was characteristic of nearly all the sergeants that played this game. They revealed high levels of loyalty, but truthfulness was weak as a value. (Of course, there were some exceptional sergeants that would have been better officers by nature.)

The reactions of officers in the officer leadership retreats were entirely different. As the behavior of the officers in power became more abusive, the officers under domination became increasingly active and alert to their responsibility to deal with the unfair situation. They offered feedback, even though it was largely ignored. They devised strikes and defensive measures. They pulled back and would not cooperate with the abusive authority. They often tried to continue to confront the abusive group or, alternately, to negotiate a more just situation.

In nearly all cases, the group in authority would become increasingly authoritarian and created more rules strictly for their own benefit and to keep the rebels in line. The abusive group would often say that the other officer groups were not playing fairly when they rebelled, withdrew, or failed to cooperate.

In other words, the group with authority became blind to its abusive nature and blamed or ridiculed the others for withdrawing and not wanting to play the game anymore.

Not Valuing Truth Results in Blindness

Like the players of this game, blindness is characteristic of organizations and leaders that do not value truthfulness in their relationships. This is because truth telling has been stifled in loyalty-based organizations and individuals. With no one to provide honest feedback, they are often blind to their abusive behavior and honestly wonder why others are reacting to it. There is no one to tell them it is wrong to shift blame and accuse others of causing the difficulties in their relationships.

The value of truth is what keeps a local church or any organization from becoming like a cult.

Honoring the truth teller is a characteristic of Godly relationships. Dishonoring the truth teller is a characteristic of cults. Cultic behavior, which always includes blindness, will result from an overemphasis of loyalty above the truth. Leaders must understand that their own desire for loyalty may overcome truthfulness in their subordinates. They must actively cultivate truthfulness along with loyalty in their subordinates.

Different Values and Expectations

This game also revealed that different kinds of people have different values and expectations. Commissioned Officers are taught in the military that proper submission means they will speak to a superior officer with courage and candor (truthfulness) about organizational problems. Officers who will not confront their commander when necessary are poor excuses for leaders. Commanders who will not hear the honest, truthful input of their subordinates without penalty are poor commanders.

The officer type of leader expects to be treated fairly by other leaders. He expects his input to be valued and genuinely considered. When the behavior of an organization and its primary leaders do not match the officer type leader's values, he will try negotiation. If the negotiation fails, he will leave the organization and move on, similar to an officer resigning his commission.

The officer type of leader will first want to fix the organization's larger problems and will not ordinarily be silent about them. If the organizational values lean too far to loyalty (and not enough on truthfulness), this type of leader will often be seen as not being a team player and be penalized by being privately labeled as such. As a result, the organization may lose a valuable leader as he discovers the truth of how the organization actually sees him.

The sergeant type of leader will remain loyal to a fault. He will adjust to the problems and not necessarily ever speak truthfully about the organization. There is nothing wrong with this type of person; in fact these types are greatly needed in all organizations. However, in unhealthy organizations, the sergeant type of leader is valued above the officer type of leader and will be inappropriately rewarded.

The officer type of person can help an organization to deal with its problems and thereby grow. If an organization creates an atmosphere for genuine honesty and truthfulness, it will attract many of the officer types of persons and will be able to keep them. It will not lose its sergeant types either. In fact, the sergeant type of leader will be much happier, since problems will be dealt with. Loyal and truthful leaders ensure that the Church will be prepared to meet the One who declared himself to be the way, the truth, and the life.

When Loyalty Overcomes Truthfulness

Loyalty and truthfulness are two covenantal values that must be held in tension against one another. Loyalty binds us together. Truth sets us free. If one value is emphasized over the other, then serious problems develop, and both values will become distorted. If loyalty is over-emphasized, then only affirmation will be given and heard as feedback. If truth telling is practiced without love and without loyalty, it does not build but tears down. If truthfulness is considered a fundamental component of loyalty, then the organization will be built on integrity. If loyalty is considered a fundamental component of truthfulness, then the organization will have true unity and honesty.

Often in an organization, whether it is the local church, a business, or a mission organization, loyalty becomes the overriding value and begins to overcome truthfulness. This is often revealed in private actions, attitudes, and behavior rather than in the official position of the organization. Insider activity can become secretive, confusing, and mysterious. The leaders of an organization may say they value truthfulness but reveal in their actions that this is not really so. There are several predictable results when this happens:

Truth-Tellers Are Unappreciated

Individuals who strongly value honesty and truthfulness are unappreciated and often rejected as disloyal. Some people, particularly those highly oriented to integrity and truth, may not be seen as team players by those who highly value loyalty. This can create conflict in the organization between truth tellers and those who prize loyalty. The loyalty value normally wins over truthfulness in these kinds of situations because those in authority typically value loyalty over truthfulness.

When the loyalty value wins over truth, it often takes the form of suppression of free expression and dissent. This does not make the elements of truth in the dissent go away. Truth will surface again and again in different, more destructive forms, until it is dealt with properly This is precisely why political tyrants are unable to completely silence free expression and why they feel the need to silence it. The truth will find a way to express itself simply because it is the truth, and God stands behind it.

Unintentional Training of Subordinates

Every time loyalty wins over truthfulness, loyal individuals are unintentionally trained to hide the truth or to put an organizational spin on it. Truthful individuals are trained that they are not really welcome. Perceptions are created that success and promotion in the organization come by telling the leadership what it wants to hear rather than the truth. Loyal "yes men" can become valued over those who have strong individual integrity and truthfulness.

Maintenance of a False Righteousness

The loyalty-based local church or religious organization will often defend its righteousness at a high cost to the reputation of truth telling individuals. Frequently, the organization will not deal with its failures in a scriptural way. Instead, the organization may blame its failures on the person it failed, even unfairly damaging the person's reputation. The truth is sacrificed to the need of the organization to maintain a false appearance of not making any serious mistakes.

Organizational problems are defended when they are brought to light by distorting the truth and putting a confusing spin on them. In contrast, the balancing value of truth persuades all kingdom organizations to repent, confess their failures, fix their problems, and seek forgiveness of the person or persons they failed. When failures are handled in a Godly way, grace, forgiveness, and mercy flow into relationships, and healing occurs. When the organization defends its failures at the cost of the reputation of individuals, then it becomes a revolving door type of organization.

Revolving Door Organizations

Weakness in the value of truthfulness over time produces a revolving door type of organization.

Individuals come into the organization but then, after perceiving the truth, try to adjust the organizations behavior rather than adjust to the organization.

Often, after becoming disillusioned by the reality, they leave the organization. Those who do stay long-term within the organization may also prize loyalty above truth. However, because problems are hidden and often neglected, they create hidden turmoil and strife for these people as well. Hidden disunity becomes a way of life for the loyal members of the organization. They tolerate each other for the sake of the organization and its mission. Finally, open conflict and strife are the only things considered as disunity.

Key Leaders in Crisis

The revolving door organization becomes a house of cards over a period of time because of hidden problems and growing disunity. A key leader or group may have a profound interaction with the Spirit of Truth and wake up to the seriousness of the organization's hidden problems. This can create a destructive crisis between or among leaders as a key leader begins to speak the truth in a loyalty-based organization.

Truth must be highly valued, or the integrity of an organization becomes weakened and cannot maintain its membership. Loyalty and a sense of mission alone cannot keep an organization together. Truth will always be necessary for long-term success.

Reputation Saturation Points

The reputation of the organization will begin to suffer from failure to listen to the truth. Many people will go through the revolving door over time. They will know the details of the problems of the organization and the organization's capacity to hide or to put a spin on them. They may have become embittered by the organization sacrificing their reputations to maintain its own. The organizational growth stops and begins a long and steady decline because of reaching a reputation saturation point, with many people speaking badly about the organization's treatment of individuals and failure to deal with problems.

The loyalty-based organization, however, will still be blind to the real reasons for its decline. This is because it has few truth tellers in the end. Its spiritual eyes have closed, and sensitivity to problems and threats are now gone. It will offer alternative explanations and shift blame once again.

Sincere Relationships in the Church

The concept of sincerity may be the best blend of the values of loyalty and truthfulness. A sincere person is a person who, out of loyalty to God and others, speaks the truth without mixture. The word *sincere* comes from the Latin word *sincerus*. It literally means without wax. This word comes from the time when Romans were building great buildings, using marble columns to support great weight. The builders would go to the marble cutters in the quarries and inspect the columns. Unscrupulous cutters would put wax into the cracks of columns to make them deceptively appear to be solid in order to sell them.

As good builders could only use sincere columns, they sought diligently to discover the truth. A column that was what it appeared to be, solid and without wax hiding any cracks, was the only thing that would sustain the weight of the building. If a builder built a building using a column that lacked sincerity, the entire building would eventually fall, possibly bringing death and destruction to many. The parallels are evident. The Spirit of Truth needs sincere people to build the Church, people that value loyalty and truthfulness in harmony with each other.

--Dr. Roger W. Saap, from the *Internet*

Pastoral Leadership for Which the Lord is Looking

You know that the rulers of the Gentiles lord it over them, and the great ones make their authority over them felt. It shall not be so among you. Rather, whoever wishes to be great among you shall be your servant; whoever wishes to be first among you shall be your slave. Just so, the Son of Man did not come to be served but to serve and to give his life as a ransom for many (Matthew 20:25-58).

In the 34th Chapter of Ezekiel, the Lord spoke a hard word to the leaders of Israel: *"The Lord spoke to me, 'Son of man,' he said, 'prophesy to them [the shepherds]: Thus says the Lord God: Woe to the shepherds of Israel who have been pasturing themselves. Should not shepherds, rather, pasture sheep"* (1)?

In the Old Testament, the shepherds of Israel were its kings. The image of shepherding entails both caring for and governing. Both Moses and David were shepherds whom God called to be rulers. Jesus Christ is himself the Good Shepherd whom Pilate proclaimed King of the Jews.

And so the Lord spoke to the Shepherd-Rulers of Israel: *"You have fed off their milk, worn their wool, and slaughtered the fatlings, but the sheep you have not pastured. You did not strengthen the weak nor heal the sick nor bind up the injured. You did not bring back the strayed nor seek the lost, but you lorded it over them harshly and brutally. So they were scattered for lack of a shepherd and became food for all the wild beasts. My sheep were scattered and wandered over all the mountains and high hills. My sheep were scattered over the whole earth, with no one to look after them or to search for them.*

"Therefore, shepherds, hear the word of the Lord: As I live, says the Lord God, because my sheep have been given over to pillage, because my sheep have become food for every wild beast for lack of a shepherd, because by shepherds did not look after my sheep but pastured themselves and did not pasture my sheep, because of this, shepherds, hear the word of the Lord: Thus says the Lord God: I swear that I am coming against those shepherds. I will claim my sheep from them and put a stop to their shepherding my sheep so that they may no longer pasture themselves. I will save

my sheep so that they may no longer be food for their mouths" (2).

The Lord has spoken a similar word to the leaders of all the Christian faith communities in our day. We need to hear it as a warning to us as the Lord moves us into, or has us in, positions of spiritual or pastoral leadership within the Body of Christ.

The Lord said: "You are all guilty in my eyes for the condition of my people who are weak, divided, and unprepared. I have set you in office over them. You have not fulfilled that office as I would have had it fulfilled because you have not been the servants that I have called you to be.

"This is a hard word, but I want you to hear it. You have not come to me and made important in your lives and in your efforts those things that were most important to me but, instead, chose to put other things first. You have tolerated many divisions among yourselves and grown used to it. You have not repented of it, fasted for it, or sought me to bring it to an end. You have tolerated and increased it.

"You have not been my servants first of all in every case but have served other people ahead of me, and have served this world ahead of me, and have served your organization ahead of me. But I am God, and you are my servants. Why are you not serving me first of all?

"I know your hearts and that many of you love me. I have compassion for you because I have placed you in a very hard place. But I have placed you there and call you to account for it. Now humble yourselves before me and come to me repentant in fasting, mourning, and weeping for the condition of my people" (3).

In Chapter 10 of John's Gospel, Jesus says: *"I am the good shepherd. A good shepherd lays down his life for the sheep. A hired man, who is not a shepherd and whose sheep are not his own, sees a wolf coming and leaves the sheep and runs away, and the wolf catches and scatters them. This is because he works for pay and has no concern for the sheep. I am the good shepherd, and I know mine and mine know me just as the Father knows me, and I know the Father, and I will lay down my life for the sheep"* (4).

The Good Shepherd has been speaking further and continues to speak to us today about what he is doing and what he wants for his Church. "I will renew my Church. I will renew my people. I will make my people one. I am calling you to turn away from the pleasures of the world. I am calling you to turn away from the desires of the world. I am calling you to turn away from seeking the approval of the world in your lives. I want to transform your lives. I have a word for my Church. I am sounding my call. I am forming a mighty army. My power is upon them. They will follow my chosen shepherds. Be the shepherds I have called you to be. I am renewing my people. I will free the world" (5).

How are we to respond? How are we to be the shepherds that Jesus calls us to be? As always, we must look to Jesus. The secret of Jesus' success in ministry was that he only did what he saw the Father doing. In the same way, we need to keep reminding ourselves that it is Jesus who is the Good Shepherd. He is doing the work through his Spirit, whom he has sent into our hearts. Our job is to surrender to the Holy Spirit and to do what Jesus is doing - what we see him doing. What is it that the Good Shepherd is doing that he wants us to do? He tells us in his Word:

1. Isaiah says, *"Like a shepherd, he feeds his flock, in his arms he gathers the lambs, carrying them in his bosom and leading the ewes with care"* (6). Jesus wants us to gather together the new believers the Lord brings into the kingdom where we are and to carry them in our arms until they are strong enough to walk on their own. This speaks of aggressive and committed discipleship.

2. *"He who scattered Israel now gathers them together. He guards them as a shepherd his flock"* (7). Jesus wants us to be more protective of those whom he has placed under us.

3. *"I myself will look after and tend my sheep. As a shepherd tends his flock when he finds himself among the scattered sheep, so will I tend my*

sheep. I will rescue them from every place where they were scattered. I will lead them out from among the peoples and gather then from the foreign lands. I will bring them back to their own country and pasture them" (8). Many who once were in faith communities and once followed Jesus no longer do. We must go looking for them and bring them back from the world.

4. *"In good pastures will I pasture them"* (9). Protect your people from the philosophies, ideas, and values of this world that do not provide healthy food for their minds and spirits. Lead your people to the heights of praise and worship and give them good, refreshing spiritual food and drink from God's Word.

5. *"I myself will pasture my sheep. I myself will give them rest"* (10). Help your people discover God's will for their lives because in doing his will they will find rest.

6. *"The lost I will seek out, the strayed I will bring back, the injured I will bind up, the sick I will heal, shepherding them rightly"* (11). Evangelization, reconciliation, healing, restoration, and ministry of the gifts of the Holy Spirit are essential, not optional.

7. *"I will judge between the fat and the lean sheep. I will save my sheep so that they may no longer be despoiled, and I will judge between one*

sheep and another" (12). Discern the spiritual condition of your people and protect the good ones from the influence of those who would stray and go off on their own or do their own thing. Protect those under your care when they are being criticized or attacked, either by the world or by other Christians.

8. *"I will make a covenant of peace with them and rid the country of ravenous beasts so that they may dwell securely in the desert and sleep in the forests"* (13). Commit yourself totally to those under your care, even if it means dying for them. Do not be afraid to discipline those under your care with the rod of correction and the staff of the authority that God has given you. Their security requires that they know you will do this, even if they don't like your correction or discipline. Do it because it gives them security, but let them know that you are doing it in God's love, not in human anger. Intercede for your people and stand against all the forces of Satan that would attack or infiltrate your faith community.

9. *"I will place them about my hills, sending rain in due season, rains that shall be a blessing to them"* (14). Share what you have with your people when they need it - in abundance, if necessary. There should be no one in need among you, nor should any of your people have to go to the world's systems to get his or her needs met. You are to be the Ministering Body of Christ. This may mean a radical reordering of your budgeting

priorities and resources, but it is the Church's responsibility to take care of her own people. If you don't have resources to give, go to other shepherds.

The Lord said, *"I will prepare for them peaceful fields for planting. They shall no longer be carried off by famine in the land or bear the reproaches of the other nations. Thus shall they know that I, the Lord, am their God, and they are my people, says the Lord"* (15).

Jesus is echoing this same word to his Church throughout the world today. "My beloved, you are my people who stand before me now. Hear my word. I shall set my house in order. I shall purify my people. I shall purify my Church. I shall set aside the deceiver, the false prophet, and the false teacher. I shall set aside anything and anyone who stands in the way of my kingdom" (16).

"Mark down this day and remember it...call it to mind; declare it publicly. Have no fear because I am faithful to my Word and shall fulfill it. I am going to restore to my people the glory that is mine so that the world will not mock of scorn them but might know that I am God and King and have come to redeem and save this earth.

"I am restoring my people, bestowing upon them honor and glory, bringing back to them the glory that is proper to my people, and making them look again like a kingdom, the kingdom of God on this earth" (17).

Jesus is going to do this through the shepherd/leaders who will listen closely to him and do what he is doing. The Lord says, "I raise my voice, but who listens to me? I cry out, but who heeds my word? This is a time of building up and washing away. This is a time of unraveling. This is a time when I establish my kingdom, and every other kingdom collapses. I raise my voice to warn my people, and who takes heed? A cloud hangs over you; a shadow envelops you. Do you not hear my voice? There is darkness around you.

"Anything that is not built by my hands will be washed away. Anything that does not come from me will not survive. I cry out to you. Do you hear my voice? I raise my voice to save my people, and they don't listen. This is a time of building up and tearing down. I have to strengthen my people. I have to prevent my people from being torn down. This is an important time for my people. This is a day of decision for my people. This is a day of decision that cannot be passed by. I raise my voice. I call forth my people. Who will listen to me? Who will respond to my call?

"I tell you, my people; there are some who need to understand this. Ways you have responded to me in the past, that have seen you through and brought you thus far, will no longer see you through. What if I call you to something new, something totally new?

"Where there is resistance in your hearts and in your groups, lay that resistance down so that I might bring you further along. I see each of you where you are. I know where it is hard for you to change and cannot promise you that it won't be painful for indeed it will cost you. I can promise you this: I shall be with you always, and the pain is nothing compared to what I shall give you in return. What you need to lay down, what you will give up, and what you think it will cost you are nothing compared to the strength you will have when I am finished with you.

I have looked into your heart and have seen my image there. Therefore, I declare you a spiritual sacrifice fitting to me. I accept you and welcome you more deeply than ever into my heart. I see your will. I see your willingness to serve me and rejoice as I show you to my Father.

As you yourself, in your own heart, say 'yes' to every word that I have spoken to you in this place and every sign that I have shown to you of my plan and of my will, as you say 'yes,' so do I anoint you with the precious oil of my Spirit and send you forth armed, equipped, and strong to serve me in the days to come. Therefore, cast off every gloom and fear and rejoice for I, the Lord, am leading you against the foe. I am with you. You belong to me. Therefore, rejoice even in the darkness " (18).

(1) Ezekiel 34:2
(2) Ezekiel 34:3-10
(3) Prophecy given at Kansas City - 1977
(4) John 10:11-15
(5) Prophecy given at Rome – 1975
(6) Isaiah 40:11
(7) Jeremiah 31:10
(8) Ezekiel 34:11-13
(9) Ezekiel 34:14
(10) Ezekiel 34:15
(11) Ezekiel 34:16
(12) Ezekiel 34:20, 22
(13) Ezekiel 34:25
(14) Ezekiel 34:26
(15) Ezekiel 34:29 & 30
(16) Prophecy given at Notre Dame – 1976
(17) Prophecy given at Kansas City - 1977
(18) Prophecy given at Notre Dame - 1976

The Gentle Force of the Servant

"Behold my servant whom I have chosen, my beloved in whom I delight."
Matthew 12:18; cf. Isaiah 42:1-4

The theme of this message invites us to return to the roots of the Christian vocation, to the story of the first person called by the Father, his Son Jesus. He is "the servant" of the Father, foretold by the prophets as the one whom the Father has chosen and formed from his mother's womb (cf. Isaiah 49:1-6), the beloved whom the Father upholds and in whom he is well pleased (cf. Isaiah 52:13-53:12).

The inspired text gives an essentially positive connotation to the term "servant," which is immediately evident. In today's culture, the person who serves is considered inferior, but in sacred history, the servant is the one God calls to carry out a particular action of salvation and redemption. The servant knows that he has received all he has and is. As a result, he also feels called to place what he has received at the service of others.

In the Bible, service is always linked to a specific call that comes from God. For this reason, it represents the greatest fulfillment of the dignity of the creature and invokes the creature's mysterious, transcendent dimension. This was the case in the life of Jesus, too, the faithful servant who was called to carry out the universal work of redemption.

"Like a lamb that is led to the slaughter."
Isaiah 53:7

In sacred scripture, there is a strong and clear link between service and redemption, as well as between service and suffering, between Servant and Lamb of God. The Messiah is the Suffering Servant who takes on his shoulders the weight of human sin. He is the lamb "led to the slaughter" to pay the price of the sins committed by humanity and thus render to the same humanity the service that it needs most. The Servant is the Lamb who "was oppressed and afflicted, yet he opened not his mouth" (ibid.), thus showing an extraordinary power: the power not to react to evil with evil but to respond to evil with good.

It is the gentle force of the servant, who finds his strength in God and who, therefore, is made by God to be "light of the nations" and worker of salvation (cf. Isaiah 49:5 & 6). In a mysterious manner, the vocation to service is invariably a vocation to take part in a most personal way in the ministry of salvation - a partaking that will, among other things, be costly and painful.

"Just so, the Son of man did not come to be served but to serve."
Matthew 20:28

In truth, Jesus is the perfect model of the "servant" of whom Scripture speaks. He is the one who radically emptied himself to take on "the form of a servant" (Philippians 2:7) and to dedicate himself totally to the things of the Father (cf. Luke 2:49) as the beloved Son in whom the Father was well pleased (cf. Matthew 17:5). Jesus did not come to be served "but to serve and to give his life as a ransom for many" (Matthew 20:28). He washed the feet of his disciples and obeyed the plan of the Father even unto death, death on a cross (cf. Philippians 2:8). Therefore, the Father himself has exalted him, giving him a new name and making him Lord of heaven and of earth (cf. Philippians 2:9-11).

How can one not read in the story of the "servant Jesus" the story of every vocation: the story that the Creator has planned for every human being, the story that inevitably passes through the call to serve and culminates in the discovery of the new name, designed by God for each individual? In these "names," people can grasp their own identity, directing themselves to that self-fulfillment that makes them free and happy. In particular, how can one not read in the parable of the son, servant, and lord, the vocational story of the person who is called by Jesus to follow him more closely, that is, to be a servant in the priestly ministry or in religious consecration? In fact, the priestly vocation or the religious vocation is always, by its very nature, a vocation to the generous service of God and of neighbor.

Service, thus, becomes both the path and the valuable means for arriving at a better understanding of one's own vocation.

"Where I am, there also will my servant be."
John 12:26

Jesus, Servant and Lord, is also the one who calls. He calls us to be like him because only in service do human beings discover their own dignity and the dignity of others. He calls to serve as he has served. When interpersonal relationships are inspired to reciprocal service, a new world is created and, in it, an authentic vocational culture is developed.

With this message, I should like, in a way, to give voice to Jesus so as to propose to young people the ideal of service and to help them to overcome the temptations of individualism and the illusion of obtaining their happiness in that way.

Notwithstanding certain contrary forces, present also in the mentality of today, in the hearts of many young people, there is a natural disposition to open up to others, especially to the neediest. This makes them generous, capable of empathy, ready to forget themselves in order to put the other person ahead of their own interests.

Dear young people, service is a completely natural vocation because human beings are by nature servants, not being masters of their own lives and being, in their turn, in need of the service of others. Service shows that we are free from the intrusiveness of our ego. It shows that we have a responsibility to other people. Service is possible for everyone through gestures that seem small but are, in reality, great if they are animated by a sincere love. True servants are humble and know how to be "useless" (cf. Luke 17:10). They do not seek egoistic benefits but expend themselves for others, experiencing in the gift of themselves the joy of working for free.

Dear young people, I hope you can know how to listen to the voice of God calling you to service. This is the road that opens up so many forms of ministry for the benefit of the community: other instituted and recognized ministries such as catechesis, education of young people, and the various expressions of charity. Young people, in a special way it is up to you to ensure that charity finds expression in all its spiritual and apostolic richness.

"If anyone wishes to be first, he shall be the last of all and the servant of all."
Mark 9:35

This is how Jesus spoke to the Twelve when he caught them discussing among themselves "who was the greatest" (Mark 9:34). This is a constant temptation that does not spare even the one called to preside at the Eucharist, the sacrament of the supreme love of the "suffering Servant." Whoever carries out this service is actually called to be a servant in a yet more radical way. He is called, in fact, to act in the person of Christ and so to relive the same condition of Jesus at the Last Supper, being willing, like Jesus, to love until the end, even to the giving of his life. To preside at the Lord's Supper is, therefore, an urgent invitation to offer oneself in gift so that the attitude of the Suffering Servant and Lord may continue and grow in the Church.

Dear young men, nurture your attraction to those values and radical choices that will transform your lives into service of others, to the footsteps of Jesus, the Lamb of God. Do not let yourselves be seduced by the call of power and personal ambition. The priestly ideal must be constantly purified from these and other dangerous ambiguities. The call of the Lord Jesus still resounds today: "If any one serves me, he must follow me" (John 12:26). Do not be afraid to accept this call. You will surely encounter difficulties and sacrifices, but you will be happy to serve. You will be witnesses of that joy that the world cannot give. You will be living flames of an infinite and eternal love. You will know the spiritual riches of the priesthood, divine gift and mystery.

--Blessed Pope John Paul II

Servant Leadership Is an *Attitude* and an *Asset.*

An Effective Servant Leader Is the Most Valuable Asset in Any Church!

According to the American Heritage Dictionary, to serve means:

1. to be of *assistance to* or to *promote the interest of;*
2. to *provide goods and services for;*
3. to *meet the needs or requirements* of.

Thus, a Pastoral Servant Leader is one who is of assistance to or promotes the interests of the *Church*, provides goods and services for *members*, and meets the needs or requirements of *those who do not yet believe as well as of those who do.*

A Servant Leader is "we" oriented, not "me" oriented.

A Servant Leader is a "team-builder", not a "game player."

A Servant Leader is teachable, not a "know-it-all."

A Servant Leader is a giver, not a taker.

A Servant Leader is part of the solution, not of the problem.

A Servant Leader builds up people, doesn't put them down.

A Servant Leader is an encourager, not a discourager.

A Servant Leader says, "Let's try it" not "It'll never work."

A Servant Leader uses authority, doesn't abuse power.

A Servant Leader is trustworthy, not a shady operator.

A Servant Leader asks, "How can I contribute?" not "What's in it for me?"

A Servant Leader brings in people, doesn't drive them out.

A Servant Leader is under-standing, not over-lording.

A Servant Leader is pleasant to work under, not obnoxious.

--Patrick J. Hession

Toward Reconciliation, Healing, and Restoration of the Church

I am, among other things, a professional mediator. In mediation, the goal is to make sure that there is a clear understanding of all the parties' positions in the dispute so that there can be movement toward negotiation and settlement.

The most important settlement within the Church is the division that has so long plagued the Church and that has led to a multiplicity of positions without a clear understanding of others' positions. Prejudices and assumptions arise when parties do not sit down and clearly try to understand where the other parties are coming from.

The purpose of what follows is to present non-Catholic and Catholic positions as clearly and objectively as possible so that dialogue can begin or continue. Much progress is being made within the "ecumenical movement," but even that term raises red flags and suspicions among some non-Catholics. However, the Spirit of Truth whom Jesus gave to the Church will guide all those who seriously and honestly seek him if we will humble ourselves and dialogue with other believers in the interest of the unity for which Jesus Christ prayed before he died "so that the world might believe."

--Patrick J. Hession

Understanding Protestantism

When speaking of "Protestant," it is important to understand that this term does not always have the same meaning as the word "Catholic" does. Protestantism takes various forms of expressions that can be summarized under four basic headings: Liberalism, Modern Orthodoxy, Fundamentalism, and Evangelicalism.

Liberalism sought to differentiate in Scripture between the "abiding essence of the Christian message" and the myths, legends, and stories used to convey that message in the Bible. Liberals did not merely abandon the idea that the Bible was infallible. Many of them went even further and refused to accord any special authority to the Scriptures. They increasingly came to look upon the Bible simply as an ancient book that might, if subjected to proper critical study, yield some reliable data about the life of Jesus and the history of Israel.

The most radical expressions of Liberalism threw out the concept of a personal God. The less extreme Liberals continued to believe in a God who transcends the order of nature as well as works through it and to insist on the uniqueness of Jesus. The left wing of Liberalism shaded off imperceptibly into humanism, and the whole movement was infected with a strong faith in the perfectibility of man and his society. This led to emphasis on the "social gospel" that commits Christians to work here and now for the elimination of injustice and the bettering of human living standards.

The heart of Modern Orthodoxy lies in loyalty to the faith of historic orthodoxy, not because it is ancient or orthodox but because it is believed to be true. Modern Orthodoxy believes that, in the orthodox Christian tradition, we have a precious heritage of truth that must not be thrown overboard just because someone has "split the atom." Nevertheless, it is willing to understand the old truth more fully insofar as modern thought makes it possible.

Instead of pinning its faith on an infallible book, it focuses on Christ as the only completely trustworthy source of knowledge about God. To treat the words of the Bible as the words of God is to erect an idol. It is to Christ the Revealer that people must look if they wish to encounter the

Living God and hear his authentic Word to all people.

Modern Orthodoxy says that no event or teaching is to be guaranteed as authentic merely because it is in the Bible. On the other hand, the Bible is the record of the revelatory events in which God has made himself known to people. It also contains the earliest record of the response of the apostles and the earliest Christian community to these revelatory events - to Christ, his teaching, his death, and the events associated with his resurrection.

Modern Orthodoxy has not settled on any one doctrine of atonement but takes seriously the basic biblical affirmation that "God was in Christ, reconciling the world to himself." Modern Orthodoxy has retained Liberalism's passion for social justice, while learning to be far more realistic about the obstacles that human nature places in the way of achieving it.

Another distinctive feature of Modern Orthodoxy is its re-discovery of the Church, not as a convenient institution for propagating Christian beliefs but as the mystical Body of Christ. The inevitable result of taking the Church more seriously has been concern about its disunity. It is no coincidence that the ecumenical movement has received its greatest impetus from the mainline Protestant denominations in which Modern

Orthodoxy has most thoroughly displaced Liberalism and Fundamentalism.

Fundamentalism can be understood only as a strong emotional reaction against the reductionism of Liberal theology. It upholds the following as "fundamental" Christian doctrines: belief in the inerrancy of the Bible, the Virgin Birth, the physical resurrection of Jesus, a "substitutionary" theory of the atonement (that is, one that holds that Jesus died in man's stead, satisfying the requirements of divine justice through vicarious suffering for the sins of the whole world), and the expectation of a physical "second coming" of Christ when he will judge the world. Fundamentalism singled out these doctrines for defense because they were under attack by Liberal theologians bent on stripping away all "supernatural" elements from Christianity.

The cornerstone of Fundamentalism from the start was an uncompromising insistence on the "verbal inerrancy" of all parts of the Bible. This phrase meant that the Bible was totally without error, and that its very language, as well as its general content, was directly inspired by God. Belief in the "verbal inerrancy" of the Bible is based on logic very similar to that which Catholics use in defending the concept of papal infallibility. God could not take a chance on people misunderstanding the self-revelation that he accomplished through the history of Israel and supremely in the life, death, and resurrection of

Jesus Christ. Therefore, he inspired the writers of the Bible to set down a wholly accurate, completely dependable record. His "superintendency" of writing the Bible extended to the very choice of words. Thus, the Bible must be revered as "the Word of God" in a quite literal sense.

It should be pointed out that belief in the Bible's infallibility is not the same thing as "taking the Bible literally." The Fundamentalist recognizes that there is poetic and allegorical language in the Bible and that Jesus himself often used vivid figures of speech. What the Fundamentalist tries to do is to follow the "natural" meaning of each scriptural passage. When the Bible claims to be recording factual history - as it unquestionably does, for example, in the accounts of the resurrection - the Fundamentalist takes it as literally "God's truth."

Fundamentalism focuses its attention on individual salvation and personal piety. It is not indifferent to the ills of society but holds that the best way to deal with them is to "change the hearts of people." It is also much preoccupied with the end of the world, the "End Times," and the traumatic sequence of "last things" that would accompany the return of Christ as Judge. Its ethical concerns often reflect a distrust of modern life and are reflected in prohibitions on dancing, card playing, and the use of alcoholic beverages and tobacco.

Many of the modern heirs of the Fundamentalist movement prefer to be called "Evangelicals" or "Conservatives." One and all stand firmly on the doctrine of verbal inerrancy. Regarding themselves as the only true "Bible believing Christians," they tend to stand aloof from the ecumenical movement that is drawing other Protestants closer together and to eschew any ties with such cooperative organizations as the National Council of Churches.

--Louis Cassels, What's The Difference? A Comparison of The Faiths Men Live By, pages 63-77, adapted and edited by Patrick J. Hession

Ecumenical Theology

State of the Question

With a new sense of the contradiction prevailing between profession of faith in the one Church of Jesus Christ and the actual division in this Church, the notion of "ecumenical" theology has become the touchstone of sincerity in the theology of all denominations and in all their theological disciplines, and a criterion for the alertness of theological thought in general.

The reason is that the one gospel of Jesus Christ, which must be preached in dialogue with the world of today, the gospel of the cross and resurrection, that is, of discontinuity with the world in the matter of salvation (since Christ and not the world is our redemption and salvation), knows nothing of the non-evangelical scandal of this gospel's being preached by divided churches. On the contrary, it presupposes the unity of the Church in faith and love, something that is not merely of secondary relevance to the credibility of the gospel but is meant to be a sign through which the world may believe.

In this perspective, the divisions between the churches are a scandal that runs counter to the words of Scripture and one that all churches are bound to remove. This can only be done if the churches carry on a comprehensive dialogue with one another in which all questions of their self-understanding and their understanding of the world and the faith can be voiced and treated. There has always been confrontation and debate among the churches. Hence, the dialogue demanded today can be regarded as a continuation or counterpart of the past.

Earlier Forms

The real counterpart of ecumenical theology in the past was the comprehensive polemics carried out by the churches. The polemical mentality was due to the conviction on both sides that each alone had a monopoly of the truth, while the other was living in error. The salvation of the opponent was in danger because of the errors of which the person was victim. Since this could not be a matter of indifference, every effort had to be made to detach the person from heresy and lead him or her back to the true Church.

The claim to be the true Church was maintained by the Protestant denominations as well as by the Catholics. The conviction of being the sole possession of the truth was formulated in doctrinal articles and propositions. The truths in question were put through a process of fragmentation and isolation in which too little attention was paid to the theological context of each proposition.

Controversy, carried on with a religious intensity that regards all opponents as dangerous heretics, was concerned with defending one's own truth and refuting the adversary point by point. Secondarily, matters were often treated as essentials, while essentials were often overlooked so that misunderstandings were bound to arise by the nature of things. It was taken for granted, without critical investigation, that one's own way of thinking was correct. Thus, one's own theses never came up for discussion, and the controversialists never seem to have tried to see things except from their own point of view, verifying the saying that "what you see depends on how you look at it." This could only lead to a hardening of positions on both sides and to narrow and one-sided views.

Along with controversy, however, there was always a certain amount of irenics. There were theologians who strove passionately for peace and reconciliation between the churches and presented concrete programs for reunion. There were, for instance, the efforts at union inspired directly or indirectly by Erasmus of Rotterdam. The theologians in question kept mainly before their eyes the picture of the primitive Church and gave a large place to the distinction between fundamental and non-fundamental truths of faith.

But it must be admitted that, in doing so, they underestimated the historical importance of dogmatic decisions in the teaching and practice of the churches. This is clear from Erasmus' proposition that the dogmatic claims of the various churches should be reduced in such a way as to bring about unity. The Anglican Communion made a similar attempt in the 1920's.

Among these theologians we must also include the mystical "spiritualists," who thought that a radical spiritualization of the notion of the Church had made room for all denominations and so restored unity, though pietism is not a direct prolongation of the thought of the mystical spiritualists.

Zinzendorf regarded the confessional churches as modes and expressions of the one true Church of Christ. Hence, all denominations had their legitimate place in his Herrnhuter Brotherhood. This was his way of keeping open, on principle, a link with all churches without denying the reality of the churches.

In spite of certain differences, the "Branch Theory" of Anglicanism has certain affinities with Zinzendorf's "Theory of Modes." This theory held that all churches - or at least all churches with Apostolic Succession of their bishops – were branches of the one Church of Christ.

Creedal theology went other ways. It was concerned with the understanding, presentation, comparison, and estimation of the doctrine of the various churches. Two procedures may be distinguished here. A purely comparative method concentrated exclusively on study of doctrines, sometimes inspired ultimately only by historical interest. But there was also a "normative" creedal theology that based itself on its own church to work out criteria for judging the doctrines of other churches.

Creedal theology has had a successor in the study of denominations that is concerned with a comprehensive description of the doctrine and life of other churches. A purely historical or descriptive type may be contrasted with the dogmatic and normative studies of E. Wolf and K. Barth.

Finally, there is the controversial theology that is concerned with the theological discussion of matters that divide the churches. Where it presents itself as a basic form of inter-confessional encounter, the question arises as to whether it does not isolate differences too sharply. When these differences are seen in the light of the greater whole of what is believed, confessed, and thought by all churches, however, the ecumenical goal of overcoming them can be better and more promisingly expounded than when deliberate attention is paid to all that divides. Hence, it must be admitted that, while controversial theology is an important part of ecumenical theology, its value must not be overestimated.

The Theological Meaning of "Ecumenical"

Five different meanings have been given to the word "ecumenical" in the course of church history. Ecumenical means (1) belonging to or representing the whole (inhabited) world, (2) belonging to the Church universal or representing it, (3) possessing universal validity in the Church (the ancient Councils), (4) having to do with relationships among several churches or Christians of various denominations (the sense that the word took on in the modern ecumenical movement), (5) implying knowledge of Christian unity and the desire to attain it (the ecumenical movement). When these five senses of the word are applied to the nature of theology and the goals it serves, the following points arise.

1. Theology must remain conscious of the fact that the revelation of God in Jesus Christ and its proclamation by the Church are directed to all people. This universal aspect obliges theology not to confuse the findings of Western theology with

the revelation in Jesus Christ. Thus, the way is open for other regions of culture to articulate their understanding of revelation in their own concepts and their own languages. The way is open to real pluralism in theology.

2. Such a plurality of theologies would be sustained by the one Church and would be established in the certain knowledge that theology is always a function of the Church and has its living roots there. The true task of theology is to assimilate comprehensively the revelation that comes in Jesus Christ. It if is to do this properly when confronted with the questions of a highly differentiated modern world, there must be a plurality of several theologies within the one Church but not a plurality of theologies of several churches.

3. In this connection, the question of a norm arises, and of the significance of the traditions of the churches. The questions arise in connection with the normative element in the term ecumenical when used in the validity of ancient Church councils and creeds. Here, the point to be made is the following: in view of the questions put by the modern world and the situation of the present day, the real meaning of Scripture (the gospel, Christ) must be propounded in such a way that it can be heard and grasped. In this process of interpretation, the supreme norm, and hence the norm of all other norms, is Scripture, of which the inmost center and central content is Christ and his

work of salvation.

It is in the light of this central message, and only with reference to it, that the traditions of the various churches and even their common tradition are to be interpreted. The dogmatic tradition of the churches, interpreted in this way and in no other way, but amenable in fact to such interpretation, must be integrated into the truth of the gospel for our own days.

4. The process of re-interpreting the message of the gospel for our own day, into which the tradition of the churches is integrated, can only succeed if the churches are engaged in a comprehensive dialogue with one another. They must allow themselves to be determined exclusively by the Word of God and the question of the present time.

5. This dialogue about the heart of the matter and the effort to solve outstanding questions in the light of the common faith will also help to solve the ecclesiological question of Church unity. Hence, an ecumenical theology understood in this sense will not be exclusively concerned with the question of unity of the Church. It will rather consider itself as a way to unity in the most comprehensible sense.

Conclusions

It follows that ecumenical theology, in the sense

outlined above, is not a new special discipline along with other theological disciplines. It is, rather, a structural element and a dimension of all theology in all its disciplines. It is impelled by the question of the division in faith and its possible elimination.

It does not simply accept division as a fact that it tries to explain by a theology of history. It sees division as a challenge to overcome divisions "so that the world may believe."

Then, ecumenical theology is a theology of fellowship, a theology that has discovered that what is common is proportionally much greater than the differences and divergences, these being only properly known and estimated in the perspective of the common faith. Thus, new possibilities of encounter and openness are created. This new openness makes ecumenical theology a theology of mutual understanding that is not merely concerned with understanding others but also strives vigorously to propound its own faith and its own understanding of the faith in such a way that they can be understood by others, in spite of different propositions, in the framework of their theology.

Further, ecumenical theology is a theology of the sources and the origins. It is concerned with Scripture and its relevant preaching today.

Finally, ecumenical theology is a theology of

dialogue and is, therefore, aware of the fact that God is constantly engaged in dialogue with mankind and that we are addressing in every person the eternal You of God. A God who does not speak is a dead God, and a Church that remains aloof from dialogue testifies only to the death of God because what it preaches - the word of God that demands to be heard and answered - would no longer be a living word.

This reminds all the churches that only dialogue among the churches, carried on in, with, and under the Word of God, the common dialogue of the churches with the world of today, can really help them to accomplish the true task of the Church in accordance with the gospel.

--Heinrich Beck, Encyclopedia of Theology, pages 419-424, edited by Patrick J. Hession

Toward A Dialogue: Understanding Positions

Similarities and Differences

What unites Catholics and Protestants is incomparably more extensive than what separates them. Both acknowledge Jesus Christ as their Lord and Savior. They also share the basic theological affirmations of Christianity that are spelled out in the New Testament and the ancient creeds. Both acknowledge the continuing presence of the Holy Spirit in the Christian community. Both look upon the Bible as a divinely inspired book through whose pages the authentic Word of God can be heard afresh by every generation. Both believe in the forgiveness of sins, the efficacy of baptism, and the promise of everlasting life to those who place their trust in Christ.

Grace

Grace, for Protestants generally, is an attribute *of* God rather than a gift *from* God. It is a shorthand term signifying God's determination to love, forgive, and save his human children, however little they deserve it. While not disagreeing with this, Catholics see grace as a supernatural power that God dispenses, primarily through the Church and its sacraments, to purify souls of naturally sinful human beings, to render them capable of holiness.

Faith

For Catholics, faith means giving full and unreserved assent to doctrines that have been defined by the Church as divinely revealed truth and to live out those doctrines in daily life and practice. For Protestants, faith is a "reckless confidence" in the goodness of God. It is more a matter of placing your trust *in* God than of believing certain propositions *about* God. Here again, there is not much difference in practice between Catholics and Protestants, but the whole Protestant Reformation grew out of the differing definitions of grace and faith outlined above.

Salvation

For Protestants, salvation is a free gift that a gracious God bestows on people through Jesus Christ without their doing anything to merit or deserve it. Here there is agreement between Catholics and Protestants and is the basis and justification for the practice of infant baptism by Catholics and most Protestants.

Justification

"Justification by grace through faith alone" became the slogan of the Reformation and has remained the cardinal principle of Protestant theology until this day. Since the Council of Trent (A.D. 1545-1563), it has been official Catholic teaching that sinful human beings are justified in the eyes of God, that is, saved, by faith and good works, which are faith put into action, as James explains in his Epistle. The whole Christian life rests on faith. Without faith, the "works," or actions of Christian living, would be without Christian value. Faith, however, itself cannot be the source of a person's salvation unless it is a *living* faith, that is, a faith that flowers in hope and love, and hence in the works of a Christian life of service to God and neighbor.

Authority

How does the Protestant know what Christ is like, what he has taught, commanded, and promised? What is the Protestant's authority for holding any particular belief?

The Reformers' answer was "sola scriptura": the Bible is the sole and sufficient authority for all Christian doctrine. However, Protestants have no authoritative guide to the *interpretation* of scriptural passages that may be obscure or confusing. Every person is his or her own ultimate authority on the Bible. This is the so-called "principle of private interpretation." On the one hand, it has served as the final guarantee of freedom of conscience among Protestants. From it has grown the Protestant emphasis on the right - and inescapable responsibility - of each human being to think through his or her own beliefs and to make his or her own decision for or against Christ. On the other hand, it has led to the fragmentation of Protestantism into more than two hundred denominations and sects. Ever since the Reformation, Protestant churches have been splitting apart because of disagreements over interpretations of the Bible.

Authority, for Catholics, resides in the teaching authority of the Magisterium, the bishops united with the Pope as a college that succeeded the college of apostles established by Jesus Christ himself. Before concluding his ministry on earth, Jesus established the Church to preserve his teachings and to carry on his work among people.

He gave the apostles full power and authority over the Church and, within the "college" of apostles, vested supreme authority in St. Peter. This power and authority exists in the *office* of the apostle, not in the person. To make sure that his message could never be lost or distorted, Christ sent the Holy Spirit to protect the Church from error. This protection is so effective that the Church's *formal* pronouncements on *essential* matters of faith and morals are considered infallible; hence, they must be accepted as equal to the very words of God.

Duly consecrated bishops in every generation are "successors" to the office of the original apostles and inherit all the powers of that office. St. Peter's supreme authority has passed down to his successor as Bishop of Rome, or Pope (which means simply *papa* or *father*). The whole "college" of bishops has a right by the mandate of Christ to share with the Pope in the exercise of supreme authority in the Church. Yet, the Pope remains supreme and *can* do on his own authority anything that he could do in union with his fellow bishops. This specifically includes the promulgation of "infallible" dogmas. However, Popes are presumed to be infallible *only* when they solemnly define issues of faith and morals for the guidance of the whole Church. They can be wrong about such things as politics and the weather. Also, only the Pope can approve the appointment of bishops and gives them the *jurisdiction* to exercise their office.

This concept of authority has the great advantage of providing a clear-cut answer to questions when Christians disagree about the teaching of Christ or the will of God. Who has the last word? This is a question that Protestantism has never settled. Considering the security in matters of faith and morals that it provides to believers, and considering the multiplicity of divisions over interpretations of the Bible as the sole rule of faith, one may wonder why it has been, and continues to be, such an issue to those who are not Catholic.

The Bible itself was the fruit of oral preaching, letters, and traditions that were circulated in the Church for many years before they were written down. The New Testament expressly says that there were "other things" that Jesus said and did that were not included in the Gospel accounts. These *traditions*, or things handed down in the Church for centuries, may also be considered vehicles of divine revelation.

Catholics are required as a basic point of obedience to accept any particular passage of Scripture as the infallible teaching authority of the Church has interpreted it. In reality, only seven passages have been definitely interpreted. Even in these few cases, the Church is only defending traditional doctrine and morals. Except for these seven brief passages, Catholics enjoy great freedom in interpreting the Bible. The Church confidently trusts that the one and the same Holy Spirit, who inspired all who wrote and assembled the Bible, continues to guide and direct it in every generation. "Faith seeking understanding" has been the motto of Christian scholarship from the beginning.

Mary

Catholics are constantly and falsely accused of "worshiping" Mary, the mother of Jesus, when, in truth, all they do is honor her as people would any mother. After all, did not the angel address her as the "most favored one?" And doesn't Scripture say that all generations would call her blessed. If people do not consider it improper to honor earthly mothers, and even have a special Mother's Day, should not Christians all the more honor the mother of our Lord and Savior for her part in bringing him to the earth and walking with him even to the cross, especially since all the other disciples ran away except John? Should not Protestants honor Mary much more than they do and seek to more deeply understand her role?

Mary is thought of as the model, image, and ideal figure of the Church. In her humble, self-effacing obedience and complete trust, she is the prototype of what all members of the Church should be like. And in her willing cooperation with the work of redemption that God accomplished in Christ, she exemplifies the Church's mission on earth.

Catholics pray to a multitude of officially designated saints, in addition to Mary, who have the power to intercede in heaven on behalf of those who seek their help. This is based in the meaning and understanding of the *"communion of saints"* in the Creeds, the Body of Christ "praying for one another," both those on earth and those in heaven.

If it is proper for people to ask fellow believers on earth to pray for them and with them, Catholics would ask, why would it be considered improper to ask fellow believers in heaven to pray for them and with them?

Sacraments

By sacraments, both Catholics and Protestants mean an outward sign or action instituted by Christ as a channel through which divine help, or grace, is imparted. Catholics recognize five sacraments in addition to Baptism and the Eucharist: Confirmation, Sacrament of Reconciliation, Anointing of the Sick, Holy Orders, and Matrimony. Their counterparts can be found in many Reformation churches. The principal point at issue is whether they are distinctively Christian sacraments on a par with Baptism and the Eucharist

Baptism

For most Protestants, Baptism is a sacrament by which a human spirit is cleansed of "original sin," understood as a person's *natural predilection* to be self-centered, willful, and disobedient to God, and endowed with a new kind of life. For Catholics, Baptism is a sacrament by which a human spirit is cleansed of "original sin," understood as a condition *of separation from God*, and endowed with a new kind of life in union with God through Jesus Christ.

Catholics and most Protestants affirm that Baptism is primarily *God's* action, not man's. Fundamentalist and Evangelical Protestants insist on the necessity of a response in faith by the person being baptized. They, therefore, baptize only adults or children after a personal profession of faith. This is known as "believer's baptism."

The vast majority of Protestants agrees with the Catholic Church that infants can and should be baptized because the efficacy of the action is altogether independent of the attitude of the recipient or the credentials of the one who performs it.

Baptist theology affirms that an infant's departure from their short life on earth takes them immediately into the presence of their heavenly father, but there is no more New Testament scriptural justification for this position than there is for the practice of infant baptism. It would seem, then, that simply "dedicating" babies, while scriptural as an Old Testament practice, actually short-changes the infant because it does not result in the removal of "original sin," thereby leaving the infant as well as children separated from God until such time as the child is able to make his or her own profession of faith. For both Catholics and Protestants, what happens to infants and others who die without the opportunity to be baptized is clothed in the mystery of God's grace and mercy and must be left there.

The Eucharist

For Catholics, the Eucharist is a "renewal" or re-presentation of Christ's sacrifice on Calvary. The consecrated bread and wine *are* the Body, Blood, Soul, and Divinity of Christ in a literal sense. They retain the appearance of bread and wine, but their true *substance* has been transformed on the altar into the very Person of Christ, as Jesus meant at the Last Supper when he said "this is my Body," "this is my Blood."

Most Protestants believe that the Eucharist is a "representation" of Christ's sacrifice on Calvary and that Christ is "really present" in a mystical and incorporeal sense every time it is celebrated without explaining how. A distinct minority holds that Christians merely perform a "memorial" rite when they celebrate the Lord's Supper.

The question may be raised that, if Catholics *are* correct in saying that the bread and wine are truly the Body and Blood of Jesus Christ, and this had been believed and taught before the Reformation and even by many of the Reformers, why should

Protestant believers then have to settle for crackers or pita bread and grape juice?

--Louis Cassels, What's The Difference? A Comparison of the Faiths Men Live By, pages 41-60, adapted and edited by Patrick J. Hession

Toward A Dialogue: Some Basics

1. From a Christian point of view, mere rejection of unity with the Catholic Church obviously cannot create a *Christian* church or any sort of unity. The same is true of Baptism pure and simple; it *alone* cannot form a Church.

2. The post-Reformation Catholic Church must at least be *presumed* to be the true Church of Jesus Christ established by him after his Resurrection until the contrary is proved. The burden of proof lies with the objector. It's historical continuity with the Church of the past is without doubt more substantial than that of the Protestant Churches since it preserves the unity of the episcopate and communion with the Roman See (which characterized the pre-Reformation Church) and since Protestant Christians themselves can only be a legitimate church to the extent that the old Church is also their Church.

3. The doctrine of the all-sufficiency of Scripture (*sola scriptura*), which the New Testament itself does not claim for itself, can certainly not be allowed to mean that the living preaching of the

Word of God did not precede the written Word of God in the Church, demanding the assent of faith and efficaciously at work in the Church before Scripture existed. Scripture objectifies the spoken word and therefore is permanently sustained by the authority Christ bestowed to the apostles to proclaim the word of God with binding force.

This is not to deny that the later Church - whose doctrine can contain nothing but the apostolic preaching and can be judged by no other standard - finds in Scripture the normative source of the truth, the permanent criterion of the necessary development of its doctrine, and the fresh actualizations which it must constantly be given. But by the nature of Scripture, this criterion is to be used as a whole nor as a decisive critical weapon with which an individual can attack the Church's interpretation of Scripture.

4. The Catholic Church also accepts the doctrine of grace alone (*sola gratia*) if it is rightly understood. From first to last, every salutary act of a person without exception is the fruit of gratuitous, unmerited favor. Everything comes from that grace which, indeed, is meant for all but which none can claim as a right. A person cannot boast of this grace as his or her possession.

One hopes in faith that he or she possesses it but can never be certain that he or she does. Daily tempted and sinning, a person flees anew to God's mercy ("Lord, have mercy on me, a sinner!")

because he or she never knows for certain whether the temptations and sins that he or she hopes are venial or minor may not forbade or conceal a real rejection of God. Thus, even the Catholic Christian admits that he or she is a sinner while clinging to God's grace as a grace that alone can save him or her. This is the purpose of the sacrament of Reconciliation.

At the same time, because grace truly transforms the justified, whatever a person does in the Spirit of God deserves the reward of eternal life - gains that merit of which Scripture is eloquent. This is a statement of fact in praise of divine grace and not a statement of Christian motivation. In order to find God, one must love him for his own sake and not simply be preoccupied with one's own blessedness.

5. Most Protestants acknowledge that there are sacraments or ordinances in the Church, that is, words that, when spoken by the Church in a sacred rite, issue into act in the individual's concrete religious situation. What is proclaimed becomes real in that individual by God's action (Baptism, Lord's Supper).

On the other hand, as Catholic dogma affirms, there is agreement that the sacraments vary in rank and dignity, are not all equally necessary, and, needless to say, do not bring about in adult persons what they validly pledge unless they are received by or produce a repentant believer.

Protestants affirm that God's word spoken by the Church is not a mere abstract statement but the actual happening of what it announces. Therefore, it is difficult to see why Protestants should not agree with the Catholic Church that all those words in which the Church engages its whole being as the sign of the fulfilled promise of grace and pledges God's grace to the individual at decisive moments in his or her life, should be called sacraments.

This is so especially since the words of forgiveness addressed to the sinner (Matthew 16:18; John 20:23), the bestowal of the Spirit by Confirmation (Acts 8), the anointing of the sick (James 5), the transmission of office by the laying on of hands (Acts 6), are well attested in Scripture, and St. Paul considers marriage to be a token of Christ's redemptive love for his Church (Ephesians 5).

6. If Protestant theology does not wish to transform the Church, which is a tangible reality in the world confessing Christ its Lord before the world, into a purely invisible, spiritual community of grace (which is not generally the case today at least); if *this* Church, despite all weaknesses and betrayals, has received the promise that the might of grace will always defend it against the powers of death and hell; if *this* Church, in order to be such, must exhibit a certain order and organization, that is, office invested with Christ's authority (however that office and authority may

be interpreted in detail); then this Protestant theology must acknowledge that, when this Church repudiates with all its strength unbelief or false belief that would dissolve its very being, founded as it is on personal faith in the apostolic preaching of Christ, it must be able to pronounce a "No" that is absolutely final and permanently binding, though it must always fall short of the fullness of lived witness to Christ, and that this "No," if it is not to dissolve the Church as true witness to Christ, must be kept from going astray by the power of the Spirit, that is to say, it must be "infallible."

Protestant theology must also recognize that this Magistral "No" must be pronounced by appointed office in the Church if it is really to speak in Christ's name and by his commission. If this office of the Church is permanently organized in a college that succeeds by right to the apostolic college, under a personal head who perpetuates the office of Peter in the apostolic college, then this supreme authority (the universal episcopate in the Church and its personal head) must be invested with the power to pronounce "infallible" judgment in matters of faith when it acts on behalf of the Church as a whole in the authority of Christ.

In other words, if the Church, whose faith is always threatened, is also constantly protected by a grace, must constantly announce new historical articulations of the faith, and if its authority is vested in certain persons, then there must be a supreme teacher in the Church whom the divine mercy preserves from error when he engages his full authority as supreme teacher of the Church.

That Church that existed both before and after the Reformation must at least be *presumed* to have been founded by Christ and has definitively made its own this conception of the permanent Petrine office, which, at any rate, is no more unscriptural than the doctrine of the infallibility of Scripture.

It is the Catholic's and the Church's duty continually to rethink and pray over its interpretation of the faith and to elaborate it, asking what it is about Catholicism that makes it difficult or impossible for other Christians of good will to recognize it as the pure, complete development of that Christian faith that they also profess and practice.

On the other hand, it is obviously the duty of non-Catholic Christians not to attempt to justify the old separation by constantly devising new and more complicated theological formulas but to consider how their own convictions can be expressed so that the old Church – which, after all, is their mother Church - may recognize these as deeper insights into its own faith.

The Catholic Church must fully realize that *unity of faith* and unity of the Church *in and under the primacy of Peter* does not mean *uniformity in discipline and theology* for the churches to unite.

--Karl Rahner, Encyclopedia of Theology, pages 1289-1292, edited by Patrick J. Hession

Jesus Christ's Vision and Order for His Church - Part I

The Foundation of the Church

"Why do you call me, 'Lord, Lord,' but do not do what I command? I will show you what someone is like who comes to me, listens to my words, and acts on them. That one is like a person building a house who dug deeply and laid the foundation on rock. When the flood came, the river burst against that house but could not shake it because it had been well built" (Luke 6:46-48).

"No one can lay any foundation other than the one that is there, namely Jesus Christ" (1 Corinthians 3:11).

"He (God) has put all things beneath his (Christ's) feet and gave him as Head over all things to the Church, which is his Body, the fullness of the one who fills all things in every way" (Ephesians 1:22 & 23).

"Living the truth in love, we should grow in every way into him who is the Head, Christ, from whom the whole Body, joined and held together by every supporting ligament , with the proper functioning of each part, brings about the Body's growth and builds Itself up in love" (Ephesians 4:15 & 16).

Jesus Lays the Foundation through Gifted Ministers

"So, then, you are no longer strangers and sojourners, but you are fellow citizens with the holy ones and members of the household of God (1 Timothy 3:15), built upon the *foundation of the apostles and prophets*, with *Christ Jesus* himself as *the capstone*. Through him, the whole structure is held together and grows into a temple sacred in the Lord. In him, you also are being built together into a dwelling place of God in the Spirit" (Ephesians 2:21 & 22, *italics mine*).

"But grace was given to each of us according to the measure of Christ's gift. Therefore, it says: 'He ascended on high and took prisoners captive. He gave gifts to men.' And he gave some as apostles, others as *prophets*, others as *evangelists*, others as pastors and teachers'" (Ephesians 4:7 & 8, 11, *italics mine*).

"Now, you are Christ's Body and individually

parts of it. Some people God has designated in the Church to be, *first, apostles, second, prophets, third, teachers*, mighty deeds, then gifts of healing, assistance, administration, and various kinds of tongues. Are all apostles? Are all prophets? Are all teachers? Do all work mighty deeds? Do all have gifts of healing? Do all speak in tongues? Do all interpret?" (1 Corinthians 12:27-30, *italics mine*).

The Purpose and Function of the Gifted Ministers

"To equip the holy ones for the work of ministry, for building up the Body of Christ, until we all attain to the unity of faith and of knowledge of the Son of God, to mature manhood, to the extent of the full stature of Christ" (Ephesians 4:12 &13).

Jesus Christ's Vision and Order for His Church – Part II

"The *eleven disciples* went to Galilee, to the mountain to which Jesus had ordered them. Then Jesus approached and said to *them*, "All power in heaven and on earth has been given to me. Go, therefore and make disciples of all nations, baptizing them in the name of the Father, and of the Son, and of the Holy Spirit, teaching them to observe all that I have commanded you. And behold, I am with you always, until the end of the age" (Matthew 28:16, 18-20, *italics mine*).

"Are you familiar with Christian teachings?"

"Yes, quite familiar, though I find that many Christians are not. I have found very few who really know Jesus in any depth, which is sad because he really is the Christian religion, not theology or the Bible."

"That is a remarkable observation, Joshua. How do you mean that the Bible is not the Christian religion? Do you not look upon the Bible as the rule of the Christian faith?"

"No, Jesus is the rule of the Christian faith."

"But do we not get to know Jesus and his teachings through study of the Bible?"

"That is one way, but Jesus never told anyone to write a Bible. The early Christian teachers wrote the New Testament part of the Bible, so it shares only as much authority as the early Church had to write it.

"Jesus gave authority to the apostles and to those upon whom the apostles would lay their hands in imparting their authority. Jesus committed his message to them. They are and always will be the rule of faith in Jesus' mind. The New Testament is an expression of a part of their teaching.

"In keeping with his promise to send the Holy Spirit, Jesus has been guiding the apostles through the centuries in an ever-deepening understanding of his message. To go back to the book alone is to deny the Holy Spirit's two thousand years of guidance and all the growth in understanding that has taken place in those two thousand years."

One of the elders commented, "But when Church leaders of the past have led such scandalous lives, don't you think people were justified in going off on their own, out of loyalty to Jesus?"

"Would Paul have been loyal to Jesus if, because he disagreed with Peter on important matters, he went off and started his own religion, saying, 'I alone am worthy to spread the gospel because Peter is a hypocrite'?

"Or would Barnabas have been loyal to Jesus if he started his own religion because he couldn't get along with Paul? Jesus never guaranteed personal sanctity to the leaders of his community, only that he would guarantee the faithful transmission of his gospel until the end of time."

"We do have an authentic authority. Elders are chosen by the community and receive their call from the community. The community gives us the authority to teach and to govern."

"Quite a democratic process!" Joshua responded. "Is that the way Jesus established the Church and the way the apostles passed on their authority?"

"Not exactly," John responded.

"Well, that should be the key to understanding the instructions Jesus gave to the apostles for the passing on of authority, if you want to be faithful to Jesus," Joshua responded.

"It is essential to follow what Jesus established

thorough the apostles. Otherwise, any group can presume to give authority to someone. But why should God be expected to honor what they have decided?

"This is a serious problem in Christianity, people making their own plans and expecting God to do what they decide. God does not work that way. People are expected to do things the way he has directed. Then they have the assurance of God's blessing and guidance."

"Joshua, you don't make it easy for us. For all these many years, we have lived this way, and now you shake our faith and suggest that what we have been doing is wrong."

"Your personal lives are still holy. You are good people, and God blesses your sincerity and your honesty. So you need not fear that your lives have not been pleasing to God."

"Are we now to find a church where these traditions are honored, do you think?"

"God is a gentle God. All he expects is your openness to his grace. In time, he will lead you where he wants you to be. In the meantime, just live out each day prayerfully. You need not be anxious."

Excerpted from "Joshua, The Homecoming", copyright 1999, Joseph F. Girzone, pages 151-153, 160-161

The Church That Jesus Established

Introduction

The reality of the Church is presupposed in the proclamation of the Gospel as the kingdom of God and cannot be separated from the whole structure from which it forms the foundation in time and place. Because of this, the experience of the Church, given as a gift of the Father by the risen Son and regenerated by the Spirit, conditions the whole of Christian reflection. The whole of Scripture speaks of Christ and the Church through the imagery of people, body, temple, house, spouse, flock, vineyard, kingdom, field, and net as well as the typological interpretation of the Old Testament.

The *"household of God, which is the Church of the living God, (is) the pillar and foundation of truth"* (1 Timothy 3:15, *italics mine*). The Church is built upon the "foundation of the apostles and prophets," with a special role for Peter, and gathers together in Christ all of Christ's disciples. The Holy Spirit makes the community of believers the dwelling place of a completely new existence and a sign of the accomplishment of God's plan for the world through Christ.

The Church is the proclamation and the presence of the salvation brought by Jesus Christ. In it, the new life of the Spirit is imparted and the apostolic faith is preserved in its memory. As the effective sign of the resurrection of Christ, the Church sees its relationship with God as the principle of salvation through the sending of his Son and as the goal of salvation through the gift of the Spirit. In the Spirit, it has the authority to interpret the Scriptures in a Christ-centered sense and communicates the Spirit to all people.

The Church sprang from the preaching of the Word, which is achieved in the sacred signs, called sacraments, especially the Eucharist. It is the fellowship of those called to Wisdom in the Spirit while awaiting the manifestation of glory.

The Church came into view, like the Incarnation and Pentecost, as the unfolding of the mystery of Christ's suffering, death, resurrection, and ascension to the right hand of the Father. It was understood to be constituted by the sacred signs or sacraments. These sacred signs are acts of Christ himself through action and words empowered by the Spirit, and are points of contact with the death and resurrection of Christ (cf. John 20:22 & 23). Thus, they are effective, when approached with a submissive and receptive spirit and attitude, simply because they are a contact in the present time with the risen Lord.

Through word and sign, the Church empowers the human race through every age and time to pass from its fragmentary existence into the unity of Jesus Christ in God, regardless of race or culture. There is, now, neither Jew nor non-Jew (Gentile), but all are one in Christ, as Paul teaches. The Church is the human race itself insofar as it must eventually come to Christ and be vivified by his Spirit. The Church is, therefore, no stranger to the life of the world. It is the human race existing in Christ and already saved by hope, living in the world but not of the world.

All authority in the Church, then and now, exists only in relation to Christ's authority and must be measured by and derived from it. It was to those whom Jesus chose and to whom they delegated their authority that Jesus said, "All power in heaven and on earth has been given to me…and behold, I am with you always, until the end of the age" (Matthew 28:18, 20b).

The authority of Jesus is passed on throughout history through those upon whom those who had received it in this way laid hands. There is no other legitimate authority in the Church apart from this authority established by Christ, its source: Christ to the apostles to those upon whom they laid their hands and so on until the "end of the age."

It is this Church, established by Christ upon the apostles and birthed through the Spirit at Pentecost, which eventually gave us the Scriptures we call the New Testament. The New Testament Scriptures themselves never claim to be the foundation or sufficiency of Christ's truth. The Scriptures are the witness of the living faith and life of the communities founded by the apostles and governed by those to whom they delegated their teaching, ruling, and sanctifying authority.

The Church that Jesus established is thus both divine and human. Jesus knew that his apostles were human and frail. One betrayed him, one denied him, and all but John left him at the final hour. Yet, Jesus promised that his Spirit would be with his Church until the end of time to preserve it in all truth. He never assured that every believer, including bishops and priests who continue in the authority of the apostles, would be sinless. Nor did Jesus ever authorize anyone to start another Church on the basis that his was flawed. He did guarantee that his teaching would not be adulterated, falsified, or lost.

Jesus prayed that his followers would be one as he and his Father are one. Disunity within the Body of Christ is not his will. Christ continues to be present by the Spirit in and through frail human beings. The multiplicity of "churches," sects, and denominations are the result of men's rebellion and refusal to accept the Church as Jesus established it, with all its sin and imperfection. In God's eyes, denominations are abominations!

There can be only one Church - the one Jesus established. All others must be seen, therefore, as man-made, incomplete in origin and foundation, birthed through a seed of division, and each bearing the fruit of further division after its own kind, claiming an authority that was not received from Jesus, whatever the purpose and intent of their founders. What truth they contain and profess is valid only to the extent that it reflects the inerrant teaching of his Church under the guidance and direction of the Spirit (such as through the Councils).

The Church as Sacrament of Salvation

The Word of God helps us to understand the Church of Jesus through a multiplicity of concepts and images. In Ephesians 3:4, the Church is seen as the "mystery of Christ" because in it is realized the eternal plan of the Father, inaugurating on the cross the union of humanity, Jews and non-Jews, in the Church and leading it to the consummation where "God will be everything to everyone" (1 Corinthians 15:28).

The word "mystery" means the act whereby God

manifests his love in the wisdom incarnate of Jesus Christ to bring mankind to glory. It is the Word of God as the fullness of revelation and is the accomplishment of the "secret" hidden for ages in God (cf. Colossians 1:16; Ephesians 3:3-9; 1 Corinthians 2:6-10).

Hence, the mystery implies that the saving incarnation of Christ takes effect in the Church through the preaching of the Word and through the sacred signs, thus leading it to the glory of heaven.

The redemption of Christ calls the Church into being (cf. Ephesians 2:13-16; 5:22ff; Colossians 1:20-22) and there achieves its fulfillment as all mankind is assembled in the Church.

The Church is itself a sacrament, a sacred sign of Christ the Head's continued activity throughout history in word and action through his Body. The Church is the Body of Christ, Head and members, living and working together through the Spirit. Hence, an understanding of the Church is to be conceived in terms of the mission of the Son and the Spirit.

The Church is the assembly in which, through the action of the Holy Spirit, the past, Jesus Christ in his Passover of salvation, becomes present in view of the future of the world at the end of time, when Jesus comes again in his glory. The Church is Word and sacrament for the whole world. Because its vocation is to place the world in the presence of the mystery of Christ in the Spirit, all of its structures are completely subordinated to the mystery of Christ. The visible and social structure of the Church is, therefore, only the sign and means of the action of Jesus Christ in the Spirit. What principally constitutes the Church is the Holy Spirit in peoples' hearts. All other things are in the service of this inner transformation.

This underlines the fact that an understanding of the true nature of the Church as a sign presupposes that it is seen in all of its spiritual dimensions. In itself and by itself, it has no consistency but draws all of its substance from its relationship to Christ in whom, through whom, and for whom it is a sign. The spiritual reality that it signifies is the whole Christ, Head and members, in the Holy Spirit and growing in grace. It stands forever in dependence on the free saving act of Christ and, thus, in the Spirit. The Church is the place of the manifestation of the Lord. It is truly a sign when it allows the Spirit to center it upon Christ and not upon itself.

As mystery and sacred sign, the Church is always to be seen as proceeding from its source, which is the Trinity. It appears in the divine thought that establishes it in Jesus Christ and descends from God's presence to become the "messianic" people of God. It is sent to the scattered, imperfect, and potential people of God, the human race called to the salvation already purchased by the blood of Jesus Christ and even now permeated by the action of grace. As the bearer of the gift made to the world by God in Jesus Christ, the Church draws the principle of its universal dynamism from the Trinity.

The Church as the Fullness of Christ and of Fellowship

To think of the Church as purely a sign, however, would be to forget that it is already the reality that it serves and signifies. The true notion of the Church as mystery or sacrament necessarily implies the notion of the fullness of Christ and of fellowship.

In dependence on Christ, in whom is given the fullness of revelation of God's communication of the human race (cf. Colossians 2:9), the Church is the fullness of Christ. It is the "fullness of the one who fills all things in every way" (Ephesians 1:23) because in it is revealed and realized the mystery of God's own life, giving people fellowship in his love. In this way, the Church is defined as an extension in the human race of the life of the Trinity through the mystery of the Incarnation, or again, as fellowship in the Spirit.

The Church as the Body of Christ

In St. Paul's teaching, the idea of the Body of Christ can be understood only through the notion of mystery, fellowship, and sacrament, as has been described. His notion of the "Body of Christ" means the actual being of the Lord, the personal body of Christ, the beginning of a new creation.

Thus, when Paul applies the expression "Body of Christ" to the Church, he means the one Body that gathers within it, in the Spirit, the whole assembly of believers by means of sacred signs, primarily the Eucharist. So, it is God himself who calls the faithful together in Christ and unites them in one Body through the Spirit. That is why the unity that binds believers together, while dwelling *within* them, does not derive *from* them but is based essentially on the unity of the Body of the Lord who died and rose again.

The Church is the Body of Christ because, once brought into existence through the fellowship of the faith professed in Baptism, it is perfected through communion in the same Eucharistic bread that puts Christians in contact with the risen Body of the Savior, drawing those who believe in him into his own Body. Unity in the Church, then, is something spiritual, real, and quite unique and clearly shows the connection between the Eucharist and the Church.

Christ, as the Head, exercises absolute authority over his Body and, in the Spirit, is the vital principle of the organic unity of the whole Body. The Church now appears as a visible Body made up of people in whom are manifested all of the different graces or charisms given by the one Spirit who animates and governs the Church. It was at Pentecost that the Church was born. Thus, the foundation of the Church as fellowship and sacred sign is the Holy Spirit.

The building up of the Church in time by means of the ministries and charismatic gifts established by Christ tends toward perfect spiritual unity in Christ (cf. Ephesians 4:11-16). Through the will of Christ, its Head, and through his permanent action within it, the Church, which is both fellowship with Christ and an institution of salvation, bears within itself all that it needs to complete its construction. The ministry entrusted to the Church as a gift to be used is also one essential part of its make-up because the ministry is charged with preaching the gospel and celebrating the Eucharist, which together builds up and develops the Body of Christ.

The Church is conceived in the same line as the sacramental mission of Christ. This whole conception affirms that the entire work of the Church is a continuation of the work of Christ. This means that a sound understanding of the Church involves a study of the relations between the Church as a whole and the hierarchy, between the primacy and Episcopal collegiality, as well as a study of the theology of the Episcopal ministry, the relation between prophecy and authority, and the exercise of authority in the Church, among many things.

The Church as People of God

The Church is the People of God established by the Spirit as the Body of Christ. The Church is a growing community involved in history and affected by the weakness of its members, who always stand in need of the mercy of God. It was foreshadowed in the Twelve gathered around the suffering servant, Jesus, the tiny elected remnant destined to spread out over the whole world. It was, then, born on the Cross and at Pentecost as the People of God of the new and eternal covenant. From then on, it is constituted by the preaching of the gospel, by Baptism and the response of faith (obedience), and is established in unity through fellowship with the dead and risen Christ (cf. 1 Corinthians 10:16 & 17; Colossians 3:11; Galatians 5:28) as it awaits his return.

The newly born Church was, thus, conscious of living in continuity with Israel, whose history was interpreted in the light of the central event of the coming, death, and Resurrection of Christ Jesus.

According to Ephesians 2, henceforward the Gentiles share in Jesus, in the grace and the good news promised to Israel (cf. Acts 15:8, 24). The faith expressed through Baptism and the Eucharist is the conclusive mark of belonging to this people, authenticated by the seal of the Spirit.

So, it is in Christ, the first-born Son who embodies the complete loyalty of God to his people, that the unique People of God, from now on to be the bearer and witness of salvation, is brought into existence. This people, by virtue of its re-creation in Christ, is a free people and so must live in a spirit of freedom (cf. 2 Corinthians 3:17) as a witness to hope in final victory when Christ returns in glory.

The Church and the kingdom

The New Testament shows the connection existing between the Church and the kingdom of God but does not authorize a complete identification. The Church will become the perfect divine community of the kingdom only after the proving and sifting time of the judgment.

It is true that the Church is already, in substance, the kingdom of God but is in a state of pilgrimage in the dimness of faith. The Church is, in a sense, already present and realized, appearing now in what are the last days (cf. Mark 1:14; Acts 2:17; 1 Peter 1:20). It is the anticipated but only partial realization of the kingdom. The Church possesses the benefits of the kingdom, the inheritance, which are the fruits of the Spirit, knowledge, and glory, individually and collectively but in an imperfect manner (cf. 1 Corinthians 12:2), in "mystery" but really and truly.

But, if the kingdom denotes consummation and fullness, there is, even now in the Church, a clear and growing sense of the distance that still separates it from the glorious consummation and that explains the growing tension that must dominate it in its yearning for the return of the Savior. This midway situation, standing between what has come and what is yet to come, has a profound effect on the whole nature of the Church and explains a great number of its characteristics, in particular its crucified state. The Church is the realm of the King who is the suffering servant. Just like its Lord, it must suffer to enter into its glory (cf. Luke 24:26). That is why the Church is, here below, a pilgrim Church (cf. 2 Corinthians 8:6; 1 Peter 2:11).

The tension between the kingdom and the Church can also be understood as a consequence of the divine action that involves the whole process of salvation - call, justification, glorification - and whose final goal is the glory to be revealed (cf. Romans 8:18-30).

Conclusion

All of the images and concepts that depict the Church are, thus, seen to be mutually complementary. They must all be interpreted in the light of the mystery of God whose purpose is to establish people in the fellowship of his Son. In the light of revelation, the Church is recognized as a society of fellowship with God, the sacrament of salvation, the People of God established as the Body of Christ, and the temple of the Holy Spirit.

--Marie-Joseph le Guillou, Encyclopedia of Theology, pages 209-217, edited by Patrick J. Hession

The Source of Truth and Unity in the Church – Part I

"Remind people of these things and charge them before God to stop disputing about words. This serves no useful purpose since it harms those who listen. Be eager to present yourself as acceptable to God, a workman who causes no disgrace, imparting the word of truth without deviation" (2 Timothy 2:14 & 15).

Introduction

"When he (Jesus) had come into the temple area, the chief priests and the elders of the people approached him as he was teaching and said, "By what authority are you doing these things? And who gave you this authority" (Matthew 21:23)? Today, there are over 45,000 different, separate, and separated Christian groups in the world, with a new group starting every five days (*Encyclopedia of Christianity*). All of these groups claim to preach and teach the truth of Jesus Christ, all supposedly based on the Word of God.

The Lord spoke to my spirit once, "You could shut down 95% of the "churches" in the United States, and it wouldn't make any difference." What an indictment! I have shared this with leaders of faith communities and others, and it didn't elicit anything except a knowing nod at best. Evidently, these people think they are in the 5%!

People should rightly ask each of these groups, "By what authority are you doing these things, and who gave you this authority?" Every fellowship or faith community needs to honestly confront these questions if it is to do the work of Christ as he commanded it to be done.

If they are doing what Jesus wants, why aren't they doing it in unity with the others? If truth and unity are from Christ, why isn't it evident in his Church? We must get rid of the man-made and self-established "churches!" Part I of this series will look at what Jesus and the apostles have to say about the Church that Jesus founded.

The Word and Intention of Jesus

When Jesus was about to ascend to the Father, he said to the *eleven*, "*All* power in heaven and on earth has been given to *me*. Go, therefore, and make disciples of all nations, baptizing them in the name of the Father, and of the Son, and of the

Holy Spirit and teaching them to observe *all things* that I have commanded you. And behold, I am with you *always*, to the end of the age" (Matthew 28:18-20, *italics mine*).

In these instructions, we find the passing of visible authority from Jesus to his handpicked apostles. They were to go forth to teach, not on their own authority but on the authority of the one who possessed it and who would always be with them, Jesus. They were to teach *all things* that he had taught them, making and baptizing new disciples who would then carry on his work.

On the night he was betrayed, Jesus promised that, after he was gone, he would send the Holy Spirit, who would bring to remembrance *all* that he had taught them and would guide them into *all truth*. Thus, after Jesus ascended, the apostles and their first disciples knew what was true because they had the Old Testament, along with what the apostles said Jesus had taught them. Later believers, who had not seen or heard Jesus in person, learned about him through the testimony of the original apostles and disciples. They knew something was trustworthy because it was preached or written in a letter from an apostle or from someone who had been taught by an apostle.

The first apostle to whom Jesus gave his authority was Peter. When Jesus asked them who they said he was, Simon Peter answered, "You are the Messiah, the Son of the living God." Jesus answered him, "Blessed are you, Simon, son of Jonah. For flesh and blood has not revealed this to you, but my heavenly Father. And so I say to you, you are Peter (Greek *Petros*), and on this rock (Greek *petra*) I will build my Church, and the gates of the netherworld shall not prevail against it. *I* will give *you* the keys to the kingdom of heaven. Whatever *you* bind on earth shall be bound in heaven, and whatever *you* loose on earth shall be loosed in heaven" (Matthew 16:16-19, *italics mine*).

This is a personal delegation of authority to Peter by Jesus, different from the later delegation of authority to the other apostles. Because these verses have been the source of much controversy in the Church, (it may be appropriate to ask why this has been so unless it is a matter of jealousy or a desire for power but certainly not a primacy of service), it is important to take a very close look at them.

Simon Peter was the first in authority over the apostles. He is always the first one mentioned when they are together or the first one addressed, so the other apostles and the gospel writers evidently perceived him in this way.

In Scripture, God often gave a person a new name to indicate a new status or position. Abram's name was changed to Abraham; Jacob to Israel; later Saul became Paul. In the Old Testament, the name "rock" was used only as a name for God and never for a human being. Now, Jesus is calling Peter the Rock.

Did Jesus mean what he said, that he was delegating God's authority to Peter, or was he only speaking symbolically? A key lies in understanding the language that Jesus used.

It is important to note here that, while the New Testament was mostly written in Greek, Christ certainly would have spoken in Aramaic, the common language of Palestine in his time. In that language, the word for "rock" is *kepha*. Several times in Scripture, Simon Peter is referred to as "Cephas." What Jesus most likely said, then, was, "You are *Kepha*, and on this *kepha* I will build my Church." As a result, there is no distinction between the two references to "rock" as there seems to be in Greek.

In Aramaic, the word *kepha* has the same ending, whether it refers to a rock or is used as a man's name. In Greek, however, the word for rock, *petra*, is feminine in gender. It would have been inappropriate to give a man a feminine name, so the translator puts a masculine ending on it, and there is *Petros*. This probably is the underlying cause of the misunderstanding of this passage as Jesus intended it to be understood. One cannot argue effectively from the Greek.

The next thing Jesus promised is that "the gates of the netherworld or Hell" will not prevail against this Church, established on the faith and the person of Simon Peter. What does Jesus mean by Church? Does he mean only a nebulous, invisible, worldwide spiritual fellowship of those who are "truly born again," regardless of institution, tradition, or creed?

Millions of Christians and their leaders of drastically different traditions and beliefs are convinced that their particular fellowship or denomination is, in fact, the "New Testament" Church, the truest expression of the Church established by Jesus, and that, by implication, all others must be impersonators or, at least, disillusioned. Yet, none of these agrees on what the Church is other than somehow it is the "Body of Christ." Is this confusion what Jesus intended when he said that *he* would establish *his* Church?

On the night he was betrayed, Jesus led his apostles in prayer: "Holy Father, keep them in your Name that you have given me so that *they may be one just as we are.* I pray not only for them but also for those who will believe in me *through their word* so that *they may all be one* as you, Father, are in me, and I in you, *that they also may be in us so that the world may believe that you have sent me.* I in them, and you in me, that they may be *brought to perfection as one so that the world may know that you sent me* and that you loved them even as you loved me" (John 17:11, 20 & 21, 23, *italics mine*).

Given the shameful, contradictory disunity in the Church today, have the gates of Hell prevailed against the Church? Is Satan successfully destroying the Church of Christ through disunity? No! What Jesus asked in his prayer must be true. Therefore, *his* Church must have been established on Simon Peter, must *be* unified, and must *be still* standing strong against the onslaught of the gates of Hell even at the present time.

Finally, Jesus said to Peter, "I will give *you* the *keys to the kingdom of heaven.* Whatever *you* bind on earth shall be bound in heaven. Whatever *you* loose on earth shall be loosed in heaven" (Matthew 16:19, *italics mine*). Here, Peter was singled out for authority, later given to the apostles as a whole (John 20:22 & 23), which provides for the forgiveness of sins.

Only God can forgive sins. Jesus forgave sins by divine authority, and his authority was challenged. Jesus passed this authority on to Peter and the apostles and on to their successors, and this authority is still being challenged. Peter *alone* received this authority in a special sense, and he *alone* was promised something else, "I will give you *the keys to the kingdom of heaven.*" Was Jesus out of his mind? What did he mean?

In ancient times, the keys were the hallmark of authority. To be given the keys to the city, whose main gate was locked at night and unlocked in the morning by the one who had the keys, means to be given free access to and authority over the city. Mayors still do this symbolically (Keys to the City) even today, though the meaning of this seems to have been lost since our cities don't have gates. Peter was given the keys to the *heavenly kingdom itself!*

This symbolism for authority is found elsewhere in Scripture. Isaiah says, "On that day, I will summon my servant Eliakim, son of Hilkiah. I will place the *key of the house of David* on his shoulder. When he opens, no one shall shut, and when he shuts, no one shall open" (Isaiah 22:20, 22, *italics mine*).

Second Kings 18:18 says, "Then they called for the king, who sent out to them Eliakim, son of Hilkiah, *the master of the palace.*" Isaiah prophesied that the keys of the kingdom of Judah would pass from the king, David's descendant, to Eliakim, the *overseer of his household*. This looks forward to Jesus, the Messiah and *overseer of God's household*.

In Matthew's Gospel, Jesus the King, the son of David, gives the *keys he possesses* to Simon Peter, designating him as *master or overseer of his household, the Church*. According to Revelation 1:18, these keys are also the *keys of death and the netherworld*, which is why the gates of Hell can never prevail against the Church.

The bottom line of this, then, is the same question

that Jesus posed to his disciples at the beginning of these verses, "Who do you say I am?" (Matthew 16:15). Did he *say* the above, or was the writer of the Gospel lying and putting words in his mouth? If Jesus did say it, did he *mean* what he said or was he just trying to make Peter feel good? If he *meant* what he said, do we *believe him or not*? Or do we prefer *our own interpretation* of what he said?

The Testimony of Paul

The apostles knew what was true because they had walked with Jesus, and he had taught them. But, what about Paul's authority? He hadn't seen or heard Jesus like the Apostles had. His authority as apostle is based on his powerful conversion experience on the road to Damascus, where he heard and saw the risen Christ. But, why did the Christians, who once knew Saul as their enemy and persecutor, eventually accept his authority to teach truth and to write epistles that expected their obedience?

In his letter to the Galatians, Paul reminds his readers of the reason his gospel is to be trusted as opposed to those who were preaching a "different gospel" (v. 6). "After three years, I went up Jerusalem to *confer with Kephas* and remained with him for fifteen days. But, I did not see any other of the apostles, only James, the brother of the Lord. Then, after fourteen years, I again went up again to Jerusalem with Barnabas, taking Titus along also. I went up in accord with a revelation, and I presented to them the gospel that I preach to the Gentiles but privately to those of repute so that I might not be running, or have run, in vain.

"When they saw that I had been entrusted with the gospel to the uncircumcised, just as Peter to the circumcised, and when they recognized the grace bestowed upon me, *James and Kephas and John, who were reputed to be pillars, gave me and Barnabas their right hands in partnership* so that we should go to the Gentiles and they to the circumcised" (Galatians 1:18 & 19, 2:1 & 2, 7 - 9, *italics mine*).

Paul is here establishing to his readers that his gospel is to be accepted because his authority had been confirmed and established by the original apostles. And, this chain of authority went on. Paul tells Timothy, "What you have heard from me through many witnesses, entrust to faithful people who will have the ability to teach others as well" (2 Timothy 2:2).

Jesus passed his authority to the apostles, who passed it on to men like Matthias. Paul passed it on to men like Timothy, who then ordained others by the laying on of hands, who could then ordain others.

This is what the Catholic Church has always called "apostolic succession." A man could not just *decide* on his own that Jesus was calling him to preach and, then, go off and start his own church. He had to be tested over time, authorized, and sent by the apostles or by one of their representatives. Paul proclaims, "Everyone who calls on the Name of the Lord will be saved. But, how can they call on him in whom they have not believed? How are they to believe in him of whom they have not *heard*? And, how can they to hear without someone to *preach*? And, how can people preach unless they are *sent*" (Romans 10:13 & 14, *italics mine*). Those who are called to *share* in apostolic authority must be sent by those who *possess* apostolic authority.

Belief was based on what was *heard*, not read, since the epistles and gospels hadn't yet been written. People heard the gospel proclaimed by preachers, but not just any preachers. There were many false and self-proclaimed apostles, preachers, and teachers. True preachers were *sent* by those who had the authority to send them. A man was not authorized to preach unless and until he had been taught and sent with the apostolic authority of the Church. So it still is today.

Paul and Barnabas continued teaching and preaching the word of the Lord. Some of Paul's teaching was included in his letters that were read in all the churches he founded and that later became New Testament Scriptures. But the written letter did not supplant his spreading of the *apostolic deposit of faith* through oral tradition.

Paul tells the Thessalonians to "stand firm and hold fast to the traditions that you were taught either by an oral statement or by a letter of ours" (2 Thessalonians 2:15). The gospel message and apostolic traditions were spread *primarily* through the *spoken* word and only secondarily through the *written* word. The apostles reminded the early Christians of "the things that have now been announced to you by those who *preached* the good news through the Holy Spirit sent from heaven" (1 Peter 1:12).

Paul wrote to Timothy, "I am writing you about these matters... so that you should know how to behave in the *household of God, which is the Church of the living God, the pillar and foundation of truth*" (1 Timothy 3:14 & 15, *italics mine*). Later, he wrote to Timothy again, "All Scripture is inspired by God and is useful for teaching, for refutation, for correction, and for training in righteousness so that one who belongs to God may be competent, equipped for every good work" (2 Timothy 3:16 & 17, *italics mine*).

When Paul wrote this, the New Testament, as we know it, had not been collected. Probably most of the Gospels had not been written yet. Therefore, the only Scripture to which Paul could be referring to here was the Old Testament, the Law and the Prophets. When the New Testament writers quoted the Old Testament, they used the Greek translation, called the Septuagint. So, Scripture here must literally mean the Greek Old Testament.

Conclusions

"So then, the Christian faith was passed on from Jesus to the apostles to local preachers approved, ordained, and sent by the apostles or one of their representatives, such as Timothy and Titus, who preached or taught the people *by word of mouth* and *by writing*. Paul asserts, here, that more was communicated in his sermons and public teaching than he was able to record in his few letters that now make up a major part of the New Testament.

Therefore, it is inaccurate to conclude that only what is in Scripture, as we now know it, is essential and sufficient. Paul said we should hold to the traditions taught orally as well as written. Paul says again, "Hold fast to the traditions, just as *I handed them on* to you" (1 Corinthians 11:2). Earlier, in the same letter (4:17), he wrote, "I am sending you Timothy. He will remind you of my ways in Christ Jesus, as *I teach them everywhere* in every church." It was to this Timothy that Paul also said, "What you have heard from me through many witnesses, entrust to faithful people who will have the ability *to teach others* as well" (2 Timothy 2:2, *italics mine*).

"We did not follow cleverly devised myths when we made known to you the power and coming of our Lord Jesus Christ but had been eyewitnesses of his majesty. For he received honor and glory from God the Father when that unique declaration came to him from the majestic glory, 'This is my

Son, my beloved, with whom I am well pleased.' We ourselves heard this voice come from heaven when we were with him on the only mountain. Moreover, we possess the prophetic message that is altogether reliable. You will do well to be attentive to it, as to a lamp shining in a dark place, until day dawns and the morning star takes rise in your hearts. Know this, first of all: there is no prophecy of scripture that is a matter of *personal interpretation* for no prophecy ever came *through human will*. Rather, human beings *moved by the Holy Spirit* spoke under the *influence of God*" (2 Peter 1:16-21, *italics mine*).

It is the duly appointed and ordained representatives of Christ in the Church who gave us *both the traditions and the Scriptures*. It is the Church, through her duly appointed and ordained representatives, that gave us, and continues to give us, the sure and trustworthy *interpretation* of the traditions and the Scriptures so that we can be kept from errors that arise so many times from private interpretation.

It is these private misinterpretations and opinions that have so often led to heresies and false doctrines, both in the apostolic church and in the present day. We still see a multiplicity of opinions and interpretations, even of the same Scriptures and doctrines, among the various fellowships and faith communities today, not to mention the various cults and sects. And yet, in our pride and self-righteousness, we point fingers at one another for being the ones who are teaching false doctrines.

The same writer warns us: "There were also false prophet among the people, just as there will be false teachers among you, who will introduce destructive heresies and even deny the Master who ransomed them, bringing swift destruction on themselves. Many will follow their licentious ways, and, because of them, the way of truth will be reviled" (2 Peter 2:1 & 2).

To prevent this, the writer tells us, "I exhort the presbyters (priests) among you, as a fellow presbyter and witness to the suffering of Christ and one who has a share in the glory to be revealed. Tend the flock of God in your midst, overseeing not by constraint but willingly, as God would have it, not for shameful profit but eagerly. Do not lord it over those assigned to you but be examples to the flock. When the chief Shepherd is revealed, you will receive the unfading crown of glory. Likewise, you younger members, be subject to the presbyters. And, all of you clothe yourselves *with humility* in your dealings with one another for 'God opposes the proud but bestows favor on the humble'" (1 Peter 5:1-5, *italics mine*).

The Church that Jesus founded is still one, united by the power and guidance of the Holy Spirit who was given at Pentecost. After the first years of the Church, after the apostles and their immediate disciples were dead, after their letters had been read, copied, and passed around from church to church, how did Christians dispersed throughout the Mediterranean, Europe, and Asia determine what was true? The New Testament as we now have it was not finally completed and its canon was not established until late in the 4th. Century. We will take a look at this in Part II.

--compiled and edited by Patrick J. Hession

The Source of Truth and Unity in the Church – Part II

Introduction

Truth is not determined by what you or I think, feel, or believe. Truth is not determined by what your pastor, friends, or even so-called experts think, feel or believe. Opinions may or may not be true. Any theory or opinion is just that until it is backed up by objective evidence. Then, it becomes fact or truth. The ultimate source of all truth is God and His Son, Jesus Christ, who is the Way, the Truth, and the Life. The primary source of all truth, according to the early Church Fathers, is the Church that Jesus established upon Peter and the other apostles under the guidance and direction of the Holy Spirit. The following are presented in chronological order simply to show the consistency of faith and teaching over a period of some 400 years from the beginning of the Church.

May these voices of the past speak to open hearts, Catholic and non-Catholic alike, so that errors can be corrected and a thirst for unity can be rekindled within the Church to the glory of Jesus Christ, her Founder and Head.

The Early Church Fathers

Our apostles, for our sakes, received the gospel from the Lord Jesus Christ. Jesus Christ was sent from God. Christ, then, is from God, and the apostles from Christ. Both, therefore, came, in due order, from the will of God. Having, therefore, received his instructions and being fully assured through the Resurrection of our Lord Jesus Christ, they went forth with confidence in the Word of God and with full assurance of the Holy Spirit, preaching the gospel that the kingdom of God was about to come. And so, as they preached in the country and in the towns, they appointed their first fruits, having proved them by the Spirit, to be bishops and deacons [overseers and ministers] of those who would believe.

Our apostles knew, also, through our Lord Jesus Christ, that there would be strife over the dignity of the bishop's office. For this reason, therefore, having received complete foreknowledge, they appointed the aforesaid and, after a time, made provision that, on their death, other approved men should succeed to their ministry.

Pope St. Clement I of Rome (c. A.D. 95), *Epistle*

to the Corinthians 40-42, 44.

Pay attention to the bishop, if you would have God pay attention to you. I offer myself up for those who obey the bishop, priests, and deacons.

St. Ignatius of Antioch, d. c A.D. 112, *Letters to Polycarp* 6.

Be careful, therefore, to take part in the one Eucharist for there is only one Flesh of our Lord Jesus Christ and one cup to unite us with his Blood, one altar and one bishop, with the priests and deacons who are his fellow servants. Then, whatever you do, you will do according to God. As sons of the light of truth, flee divisions and evil doctrines.

St. Ignatius of Antioch, *Letter to the Philadelphians* 3.

Avoid divisions as the beginning of evils. All of you, follow the bishop as Jesus Christ followed the Father, follow the presbytery as the apostles, and respect the deacons as the commandment of God. Let no man perform anything pertaining to the Church without the bishop. Wherever the bishop appears, there let the people be, just as wherever Christ Jesus is, there is the Catholic Church.

St. Ignatius of Antioch, *Epistle to the Smyrnaeans* 8.

All should respect deacons as Jesus Christ, just as

all should regard the bishop as the image of the Father and the clergy as God's senate and the College of the apostles. Without these three orders you cannot begin to speak of a Church.

Do nothing without your bishop and, indeed, be subject to the clergy as well, seeing in them the apostles of Jesus Christ our hope for, if we live in him, we shall be found in him.

St. Ignatius of Antioch, *Letter to the Trallians* 2.

Papias makes no claim to be a hearer and eyewitness of the holy apostles but to have received the contents of the faith from those who were known to them. He tells us this in his own words, "I shall not hesitate to set down for you, along with my interpretations, all things that I learned from the elders with care and recorded with care, being well assured of their truth. I took pleasure not in those who record strange precepts but in those who relate such precepts as were given to the faith from the Lord and are derived from the truth itself.

"Besides, if ever any man came who had been a follower of the elders, I would inquire about the sayings of the elders; what Andrew said, or Peter, or Philip, or Thomas, or James, or John, or Matthew, or any other of the Lord's disciples, and what Ariston says, and John the Elder, who are disciples of the Lord. I did not consider that I got so much profit from the contents of books as from the utterances of a living and abiding voice."

Concerning Mark, the writer of the Gospel, he says, "The Elder used to say this also. Mark became an interpreter of Peter and wrote down accurately, but not in order, as much as he remembered, or as he (Peter) related, of the sayings and doings of Christ. He was not a hearer or follower of the Lord but afterwards, as I said, of Peter, who adapted his teachings to the needs of the moment and did not make an ordered exposition of the sayings of the Lord. So, Mark made no mistake when he, thus, wrote down some things as he remembered them, or as he (Peter) related them. He made it his special care to omit nothing of what he heard and to make no false statement therein." This is what Papias relates concerning Mark.

Now, concerning Matthew, it is stated, "So, then, Matthew recorded the oracles or prophetic discourses in the Hebrew tongue, and each interpreted them to the best of his ability."

Papias, Bishop of Hierapolis (c. A.D.130), *Expositions of the Oracle of the Lord*, Eusebius, H.E. III 39.

Let the bishop be ordained after he has been chosen by all the people. When he has been named and shall please all, let him, with the priests and such bishops as may be present, assemble with the people on Sunday.

While all give their consent, the bishops shall lay their hands on him, and the priests shall stand by in silence. All, indeed, shall keep silent, praying in their hearts for the descent of the Spirit. Then, one of the bishops present shall, at the request of all, lay his hands on him who is ordained and shall pray.

St. Hippolytus (A.D. 170-235), *Apostolic Tradition,* Part I.

The Church of Corinth remained in the right doctrine down to the episcopate of Primus at Corinth. After arriving in Rome, I made a succession down to Anicetus. To Anicetus succeeded Soter, who was followed by Eleutherus. In every succession and in every city, things are ordered according to the preaching of the Law, the Prophets, and the Lord.

Hegesippus (c. A.D.175), in Eusebius, H.E. IV 22, 2.

The Church, although dispersed throughout the whole world even to the ends of the earth, has received from the apostles and from their disciples the faith in one God.

As I said before, the Church who received this preaching and this faith, although she is disseminated throughout the whole world, yet guarded it as if she occupied but one house. She, likewise, believes these things just as if she had but one soul and one and the same heart.

Harmoniously, she proclaims them and hands them down as if she possessed one mouth. For, while the languages of the world are diverse, nevertheless, the authority of the tradition is one and the same.

Neither do the churches among the Germans believe otherwise or have another tradition, nor do those among the Ibernians, nor among the Celts, nor away in the East, nor in Egypt, nor in Libya, nor in those places that have been established in the central regions of the world. But, just as the sun, that creature of God, is one and the same throughout the whole world, so, also, the preaching of the truth shines everywhere and enlightens all people who desire a knowledge of truth.

Nor will any of the rulers in the churches, whatever his power of eloquence, teach otherwise for no one is above the teacher, nor will he who is weak in speaking detract from the tradition. The faith is one and the same and cannot be amplified by one who is able to say much about it nor diminished by one who can say but little.

St. Irenaeus, bishop of Lyons, (c. A.D. 180) *Against Heresies I, X:*1 & 2.

Matthew published his gospel among the Hebrews in their own tongue when Peter and Paul were preaching the gospel in Rome and founding the church there. After their departure, Mark, the disciple and interpreter of Peter, handed down to us in writing the substance of Peter's preaching. Luke, the follower of Paul, set down in a book the gospel preached by his teacher. Then John, the disciple of the Lord, who also leaned on his breast, produced his Gospel while he was living at Ephesus in Asia.

St. Irenaeus, bishop of Lyons, (c. A.D. 180) *Against Heresies, III, I, I,* Eusebius. H.E. v. 8.

When they [the heretics] are refuted from the Scriptures, they accuse the Scriptures themselves as if there were something amiss with them and they carried no authority Yet, when we appeal again to that tradition that is derived from the apostles and which is safeguarded in the churches through the succession of presbyters, they, then, are adversaries of tradition, claiming to be wiser not only than the presbyters but even than the apostles and to have discovered the truth undefiled. Thus, it happens that they now agree neither with the Scriptures nor with tradition.

Those who wish to discern the truth may observe the apostolic tradition made manifest in every church throughout the world. We can enumerate those who were appointed bishops in the churches by the apostles and their successors down to our own day, who never taught and never knew absurdities such as these men produce. If the apostles had known hidden mysteries which they taught the perfect in private and in secret, they would, rather, have committed them to those to whom they entrusted the churches for they wished those men to be perfect and blameless whom they left as their successors and to whom they handed over their own office of authority.

We confound all those who, in any way, whether for self-pleasing, or vainglory, or blindness, or evil-mindedness, hold unauthorized meetings. This we do by pointing to the apostolic tradition and the faith that is preached to people, which has come down to us through the succession of bishops, the tradition and creed of the greatest, the most ancient church, the church known to all people which was founded and set up at Rome by the two most glorious apostles, Peter and Paul. With this church, because of its position of leadership and authority, must agree every church, that is, the faithful everywhere. In her, the apostolic tradition has always been preserved by the faithful from all parts.

The blessed apostles, after founding and building up the Church, handed over to Linus the office of bishop. Paul mentions this Linus in his epistle to Timothy (2 Timothy 4:21). Anacletus succeeded him, after whom, in the third place after the apostles, Clement was appointed to the bishopric. He not only saw the blessed apostles but also conferred with them and had their preaching ringing in his ears and their tradition before his eyes. In this, he was not alone for many still survived whom the apostles had taught.

Now, when Clement was bishop, there arose no small dissension among the brethren in Corinth, and the Church in Rome sent a most weighty letter to the Corinthians, urging them to reconciliation, renewing their faith, and telling them again of the tradition which he had lately received from the apostles.

Euarestus succeeded this Clement, Alexander followed Euarestus, then Sixtus was appointed, the sixth after the apostles. After him came Telesphorus, who had a glorious martyrdom. Then, Hyginus, Pius, Anicetus, and Soter. Now, in the twelfth place from the apostles, Eleutherus occupies the See. In the same order and succession, the apostolic tradition in the Church and the preaching of the truth has come down to our time.

Then Polycarp, besides being instructed by the apostles and acquainted with many who had seen the Lord, was also appointed by the apostles for Asia as bishop of the church in Smyrna. Even I saw him in my early youth. He remained with us a long time and, at a great age, suffered a martyrdom full of glory and renown and departed this life, having taught always the things that he had learned from the apostles, which the Church hands down, which alone are true. There testify to these things all the churches throughout Asia and the successors of Polycarp down to this day.

Polycarp converted many of the before-mentioned heretics to the Church of God, declaring that he had received this one and only truth from the apostles, the truth that has been handed down by the Church.

Since, therefore, there are so many proofs, there is now no need to seek among others the truth that they can easily obtain from the Church. The apostles have lodged all that there is of the truth with her as with a rich bank, holding back nothing. And so, anyone who wishes can draw from her the draught of life. This is the gateway of life; all the rest are thieves and robbers.

Therefore, we ought to obey only those presbyters who are in the Church, who have their succession from the apostles, as we have shown, who, with their succession in the episcopate, have received the sure gift of the truth according to the pleasure of the Father. The rest who stand aloof from the primitive succession and assemble in any place whatever we must regard with suspicion, either as heretics and evil-minded or as schismatics, puffed up and complacent, or, again, as hypocrites, acting, thus, for the sake of gain and vainglory. All these have fallen from the truth.

St. Irenaeus, bishop of Lyons, (c. A.D. 180), *Against Heresies III* 2-4, *IV* 26, 2.

The apostles first bore witness to the faith in Christ Jesus throughout Judea and founded churches there. They then went out into the world and preached to the nations the same doctrine of the same faith. They, likewise, founded churches in every city, from which the other churches thereafter derived their shoot of faith and the seeds of doctrine, yes, and are still deriving them in order to become churches. It is through this that these churches are themselves apostolic in that they are the offspring of apostolic churches.

Every kind of thing must be classified in accordance with its origin. So, the churches, many and great as they may be, are really the one Primitive Church issuing from the apostles, which is their source. All are primitive and all are apostolic, while all are one. This unity is proved by the peace they share, by their title of brotherhood, and by their contract of hospitality. These privileges have but one ground, the one tradition of the same revelation.

It is, therefore, on this ground that we put forward our ruling, namely that, if Jesus Christ sent out the apostles to preach, no others are to be accepted as preachers but those whom Christ appointed since "no other knows the Father except the Son and he to whom the Son has revealed him." And, the Son seems not to have revealed him to any but the apostles whom he sent to preach, assuredly to preach what he revealed to them.

What they preached, that is, what Christ revealed to them, on my ruling, ought to be established solely through these same churches that the apostles themselves founded by preaching to them as well as by the living voice, as the phrase is, as by their Epistles afterwards.

If this be so, it follows that all doctrine that accords with these apostolic churches, the sources and originals of the faith, must be reckoned as the truth since it preserves, without doubt, what the churches received from the apostles, the apostles from Christ, and Christ from God. We are in communion with the apostolic churches. There is no difference of doctrine. This is the testimony of the truth.

But, if any of these [heretics] are bold enough to insert themselves into the apostolic age in order to seem to have been handed down from the apostles because they existed under the apostles, we can say: Let them, then, produce the origins of their churches. Let them unroll the list of their bishops, an unbroken succession from the beginning, so that that first bishop has as his precursor and the source of his authority one of the apostles or one of the apostolic men who, though not an apostle, continued with the apostles. This is how the apostolic churches report their origins. Thus, the Church of the Smyrnaeans relates that John appointed Polycarp, the Church of Rome that Peter ordained Clement.

Tertullian (A.D. 160-240), *Concerning the Prescript of the Heretics* 20, 21, 32.

The Church is called Catholic or universal because it has spread throughout the entire world, from one end of the earth to the other. Again, it is called Catholic because it teaches fully and unfailingly all the doctrines which ought to be brought to people's knowledge, whether concerned with visible or invisible things, with the realities of heaven and the things on earth.

Another reason for the name of Catholic is that the Church brings all classes of people into religious obedience, rulers and subjects, the learned and the unlettered. Finally, it deserves the word Catholic because it heals and cures unrestrictedly every type of sin and because it possesses within itself every kind of virtue.

St. Cyril of Jerusalem, c A.D. 350-387, *Catechesis* 18.

The third book of the gospel is that according to Luke. Luke, the physician, when, after the Ascension of Christ, Paul had taken him to himself as traveling companion, wrote in his own name what he had been told, although he had not himself seen the Lord in the flesh. He set down the events as far as he could ascertain them and began his story with the birth of John. The fourth gospel is that of John, one of the disciples.

Moreover, the Acts of all the apostles are included in one book. Luke addressed them to the most excellent Theophilus because the several events took place when he was present. He makes this plain by the omission of the passion of Peter and of the journey of Paul when he left Rome for Spain.

For the Epistles of Paul, he wrote to not more than seven churches in this order: the first to the Corinthians, the second to the Ephesians, the third to the Philippians, the fourth to the Colossians, the fifth to the Galatians, the sixth to the Thessalonians, the seventh to the Romans.

He wrote, besides these, one to Philemon, one to Titus, and two to Timothy. These were written in personal affection but have been hallowed by being held in honor by the Catholic Church for the regulation of church discipline. There are many others that cannot be received into the Catholic Church.

The Epistle of Jude and two bearing the name of John are accepted in the Catholic Church. We receive also the Apocalypse of John.

The Moratorian Canon, probably the 8th. Century. The Greek original probably dates from the end of the 2nd. Century.

It can be easily proved to the mind of faith by a brief statement of the truth. The Lord says to Peter, "I say to you that you are Peter, etc." (Matthew 16:18 & 19). [Again, after his Resurrection, he says to him, "Feed my sheep."]

He builds his Church upon one man and, though he gives to all the apostles an equal power and says, "As my Father sent me, etc." (John 20:21-23), yet has ordained, by his authority, the source of unity beginning from one man.

Certainly, the other apostles were what Peter was, endued with an equal fellowship both of honor and of favor. But, the beginning was made from unity so that the Church of Christ may be shown to be one. To this one Church, the Holy Spirit points in the Song of Songs, in the person of our Lord, saying, "My dove, my spotless one, is but one. She is the only one of her mother, elect of her that bore her" (Canticle 6:9). He that holds not this unity of the Church, does he think that he holds the faith? He that strives against and resists the Church, is he confident that he is in the Church? For the blessed apostle Paul also teaches the same thing and sets forth the sacrament of unity, saying, "There is one Body, etc." (Ephesians 4:4 & 5).

The Church, flooded with the light of the Lord, extends her rays over the entire globe yet is one light that is diffused everywhere, and the unity of the Body is not broken up. She stretches forth her branches over the whole earth in rich abundance, spreads far and wide the bounty of her onward flowing streams yet there is but one Head, one Source, one Mother, abounding in the increase of her fruitfulness. Of her womb we are born, by her milk we are nourished, and we are quickened from her breath.

The spouse of Christ cannot be made an adulteress; she is undefiled and chaste. She it is who preserves us for God, who enrolls into the kingdom the sons she has borne. Whoever stands aloof from the Church and is joined to an adulteress is cut off from the promises given to the Church. He or she that leaves the Church of Christ does not attain to Christ's rewards. He or she is an alien, an outcast, an enemy. He or she cannot have God for his or her Father who does not have the Church for his or her mother. If anyone was able to escape outside of Noah's ark, then he or she also escapes who is outside the doors of the Church. He or she that rends or divides the Church of Christ cannot possess the clothing of Christ.

Cyprian, bishop of Carthage, (A.D. 248-258), *On the Unity of the Church* 4-6.

Our Lord, whose precepts and admonitions we are bound to observe, ordered the high office of bishop and the system of his Church when he speaks in the Gospel and says to Peter, "You are Peter, etc." (Matthew 16:18 & 19). Since then, age has followed age, and bishop has followed bishop in succession, and the office of the episcopate and the system of the Church has been handed down so that the Church is founded on the bishops, and every act of the Church is directed by these same presiding officers. Since this has been established by divine ordinance, I am astonished that certain persons have been rash and bold enough to choose to write to me in such a manner as to send their letter in the Church's name, when the Church consists of the bishops, the clergy, and all the faithful.

Cyprian, bishop of Carthage, *Epistle* 33, 1

In this place (John 6:67-69, "Lord, to whom shall we go? etc."), Peter, upon whom the Church had to be built, speaks as representing the Church for our instruction. For, although the proud and arrogant multitude of those who refuse to obey may leave, still the Church never departs from Christ, and the Church is made up of the people united to their priest and the flock that cleaves to its shepherd. Hence, you should know that the bishop is in the Church and the Church in the bishop and that, if anyone is not with the bishop, he is not in the Church. Know, also, that they vainly beguile themselves who, not being at peace with the priests of God, approach by stealth and trust by underhanded means to enter into communion with certain persons. The Church is one. It may not be rent or sundered but should, assuredly, be bound together and united by the glue of the priests who are in harmony one with another.

Cyprian, bishop of Carthage, *Epistle* 56, 7.

Continue in the profession of that religion that the divine apostle Peter delivered to the Romans as it has been preserved by faithful tradition and is now professed by the Pontiff Damasus and by Peter, bishop of Alexandria, a man of apostolic holiness.

According to the apostolic teaching and the doctrine of the Gospel, let us believe the one deity of the Father, the Son, and the Holy Spirit, in equal majesty and in a holy Trinity.

We authorize the followers of this law to assume the title of Catholic Christians. As for the others, since, in our judgment, they are foolish madmen, we decree that they will be branded with the ignominious name of heretics and shall not presume to give to their gatherings the name of churches.

Theodosius I (A.D. 379-395), *On Catholics and Heretics* A.D. 380

A man cannot have salvation except in the Catholic Church. Outside the Catholic Church, he can have everything except salvation. He can have honor, he can have sacraments, he can sing Alleluia, he can answer Amen, he can possess the gospel, he can have and preach faith in the name of the Father, and of the Son, and of the Holy Spirit, but *never, except in the Catholic Church, will he be able to find salvation* (*italics mine*).

St. Augustine, bishop of Hippo, c. A.D. 418.

The universal ordering of the Church at its birth took its origin from the office of blessed Peter, in which is found both its directing power and its supreme authority. From him, as from its source when our religion was in its growth stage, all the churches received their common order. This much is shown by the Council of Nicea, which knew that all had been assigned to him by the Word of the Lord.

So, it is clear that this Church is to all the churches throughout the world as the head is to the members and that whoever separates himself from it becomes an exile from the Christian religion since he ceases to belong to its fellowship.

Pope St. Boniface I, d. A.D. 422, *Letter* 14.

I have, therefore, continually given the greatest pains and diligence to inquiring from the greatest number of men outstanding in holiness and in doctrine how I can secure a kind of fixed and, as it were, general and guiding principle for distinguishing the true Catholic faith from the degraded falsehoods of heresy. The answer that I receive is always to this effect: that, if I wish, or indeed, if anyone wishes, to detect the deceits of heretics that arise, to avoid their snares, and to keep healthy and sound in a healthy faith, we ought, with the Lord's help, to fortify our faith in a twofold manner: first, by the authority of God's Law, then by the tradition of the Catholic Church.

Here, it may be, someone will ask, "Since the canon of Scripture is complete and, in itself, abundantly sufficient, what need is there to join to it the interpretation of the Church?" The answer is that, because of the very depth of Scriptures, all people do not place one identical interpretation upon it. The statements of the same writer are explained by different people in different ways, so much so that it seems almost possible to extract from it as many opinions as there are people. Therefore, because of the intricacies of error, which is so multiform, there is a great need for the laying down of a rule for the exposition of the prophets and apostles in accordance with the standard of the interpretation of the Church Catholic.

Now, in the Catholic Church itself, we take the greatest care to hold *that which has been believed everywhere, always, and by all.*

This is truly and properly "Catholic," as is shown by the very force and meaning of the word, which comprehends everything almost universally. We shall hold to this rule if we follow *universality* [i.e. ecumenicity], *antiquity*, and *consent*. We shall follow universality if we acknowledge the one Faith to be true which the whole Church throughout the world confesses; antiquity, if we in no wise depart from those interpretations and opinions of all, or certainly nearly all, bishops and doctors (teachers) alike.

What, then, will the Catholic Christian do if a small part of the Church has cut itself off from communion of the universal Faith? The answer is sure. He or she will prefer the healthiness of the whole Body to the morbid and corrupt link.

But, what if some novel contagion tries to infect the whole Church and not merely a tiny part of it? Then, he or she will take care to cleave to antiquity, which cannot now be led astray by the deceit of novelty.

What if, in antiquity itself, two or three people, or it may be a city, or even a whole province be detected in error? Then, he or she will take the greatest care to prefer the decrees of the ancient General Councils, if there are such, to the irresponsible ignorance of a few people.

But, what if some error arises regarding which nothing of this sort is to be found? Then, he or she must do his or her best to compare the opinions of the Fathers and inquire into their meaning, provided always that, though they belong to diverse times and places, they, yet, continued in the faith and communion of the one Catholic Church; and let them be teachers approved and outstanding. Whatever he or she finds to have been held, approved, and taught, not by one or two only but by all equally and with one consent, openly, frequently, and persistently, let him or her take this as to be held without the slightest hesitation.

St. Vincent of Lerins, A.D. 434, *The Vincentian Canon (italics mine)*.

Keep that which is committed. What is committed? It is that which has been entrusted to you not that which you have invented, what you have received not what you have devised, not a matter of ingenuity but of doctrine, not of private acquisition but of public interpretation, a matter brought to you not created by you, a matter you are not the author of but the keeper of, not the teacher but the learner, not the leader but the follower.

Guard this deposit. Preserve the talent of the Catholic Church inviolate and unimpaired. What has been entrusted to you may remain with you and may be handed down by you. You received gold; hand it down as gold.

The question may be asked, "If this is right, then is no progress of religion possible within the Church of Christ? To be sure, there has to be progress, but it must be progress in the proper sense of the word and not a change in faith. Progress means that each thing grows within itself, whereas change implies that one thing is transformed into another.

The growth of religion in the soul should be like the growth of the body that, in the course of years, develops and unfolds yet remains the same as it was. The course of years always completes in adults the parts and forms with which the wisdom of the Creator has previously imbued infants.

In the same way, the dogma of the Christian religion ought to follow these laws of progress so that it may be consolidated in the course of years, developed in the sequence of time, and sublimated by age, yet remain incorrupt and unimpaired, complete and perfect in all the properties of its parts and all its essentials so that it does not allow of any change, or any less of its specific character, or any variation in its inherent form.

St. Vincent of Lerins (c. A.D. 445), *A Commentary for the Antiquity and Universality of the Catholic Faith against the Profane Novelties of All Heresies* 22.

We are convinced that the only defense for us and for our Empire is in the favor of the God of heaven. In order to deserve this favor, it is our first care to support the Christian Faith on its venerable religion.

Therefore, inasmuch as the pre-eminence of the Apostolic See is assured by the merit of St. Peter, the first of its bishops, by the leading position of the City of Rome, and also by the authority of the holy Synod, let not presumption strive to attempt anything contrary to the authority of that See. For the peace of the churches will only then be everywhere preserved when the whole Body acknowledges its ruler.

Hitherto, this has been observed without violation. Nothing shall be attempted contrary to the ancient custom without the authority of the venerable pope of the Eternal City. Whatsoever the authority of the Apostolic See has enacted, or shall enact, let that be held as law for all.

The Edict of Valerian III, A.D. 445.

--compiled and edited by Patrick J. Hession

The Source of Truth and Unity in the Church – Part III

Introduction

"Remain faithful to what you learned and believed because you know from whom you learned it, and that from infancy you have known the sacred Scriptures, which are capable of giving wisdom for salvation through faith in Christ Jesus. All Scripture is inspired by God and is useful for teaching, for refutation, for correction, and for training in righteousness so that one who belongs to God may be competent, equipped for every good work" (2 Timothy 3:14-17).

As we have already seen, this Scripture of which Paul is speaking must be the Old Testament, since the New Testament had not yet been written nor its canon authentically established. This quotation furnishes no argument whatever that the Sacred Scriptures, without Tradition (which means simply the oral preaching, teaching, and practice of the early Church that has been "handed down"), is the sole rule of faith. The Scripture is useful; it is not said to be sufficient. The apostle himself requires the help of Tradition: "So brethren, stand firm and hold fast to the traditions that you were taught, either *by an oral statement* or *by a letter of ours*" (2 Thessalonians 2:15, *italics mine*). This has all been established in Parts I and II.

The most important evidence that the Catholic Church is the one that Jesus Christ established, then, must be based on its continuity with the apostolic teaching, reflected in both the oral and written tradition of the apostles and their disciples and in the teaching and preaching of the early Church Fathers.

As we saw in Part II, St. Vincent of Lerins summarized this as "That which has been believed everywhere, always, and by all." He also set forth a threefold test of legitimate inquiry: universality, antiquity, and open, frequent, and persistent consent (Vincent of Lerins, *The Vincentian Canon*, 434).

Ever since the schism of the Eastern Church in 1054, and especially since the Reformation, no faith community, sect, or cult, whether liturgical or fundamentalist/evangelical, has claimed this continuity except the Catholic Church, whose See is in Rome and which includes Eastern Rite churches in union with it, and the Eastern Orthodox. The closest exception was the Church of England in 1920.

Ever since Martin Luther dubbed the Catholic Church the "Whore of Babylon," and the *Westminster Confession of Faith* of 1643 called the Pope "that Antichrist, the man of sin, and son of perdition that exalts himself in the Church against Christ and all that is called God," many others have uttered these and other slanderous accusations as from the mouth of a parrot, without serious and open-minded analysis or thought.

Perhaps, it is time for an objective review of this Church, first to see what it really teaches and, then, whether what it teaches is in continuity with the criteria set down by St. Vincent of Lerins above.

Many who condemn the Church of Rome do so without ever having taken the time or made the effort to study seriously what it really teaches and believes. Hopefully, the following will provide the opportunity for those who are open and not already convinced by pre-conceived ideas, misinformation, and prejudices passed on by their own teachers and preachers or their own lack of study.

The Transmission of Divine Revelation

God has revealed himself fully by sending his own Son, in whom he has established his New Covenant forever. The Son is his Father's definitive Word. There will be no further Revelation after him.

"God wills everyone to be saved and to come to knowledge of the truth" (1 Timothy 2:4), that is, of Christ Jesus (cf. John 14:6). Christ must be proclaimed to all individuals and nations so that this revelation may reach to the ends of the earth. God graciously arranged that all things he had once revealed for the salvation of all peoples should remain in their entirety throughout the ages and be transmitted to all generations (cf. 2 Corinthians 1:20; 3:16-4:6).

Christ the Lord, in whom the entire Revelation of the Most High God is summed up, commanded the apostles to preach the Gospel that had been promised beforehand by the prophets and that he fulfilled in his own person and promulgated with his own lips. In preaching the Gospel, they were to communicate the gifts of God to all people. This Gospel was to be the source of all saving truth and moral discipline (cf. Matthew 28:19 & 20; Mark 16:15).

In keeping with the Lord's command, the Gospel was handed on in two ways:

--*orally* by the apostles who handed on, by the spoken word of their preaching, by the example they gave, by the institutions they established, what they themselves had received, whether from the lips of Christ, from his way of life and his works, or learned at the prompting of the Holy Spirit;

--*in writing* by those apostles and other men associated with the apostles who, under the inspiration of the same Holy Spirit, committed the message of salvation to writing.

In order that the full and living Gospel might always be preserved in the Church, the apostles left bishops, or overseers, as their successors. They gave them their own teaching authority (cf. St. Irenaeus, *Against Heresies* 3, 3, 1 in Part II). Indeed, the apostolic preaching, which is expressed in a special way in the inspired books, was to be preserved in a continuous line of succession until the end of time (cf. Acts 20:28; St. Clement of Rome, *Epistle to the Corinthians* 42, 44 in Part II).

This living transmission, accomplished in the Holy Spirit, is called Tradition since it is distinct from Sacred Scripture, though closely connected to it. Through Tradition, the Church, in her doctrine, life, and worship, perpetuates and transmits to every generation all that she herself is and all that she believes (cf. St. Irenaeus, *Against Heresies* 1, 10, 1-2; 5, 20, 1).

The Father's self-communication, made through his Word in the Holy Spirit, in a way that the two cannot be separated so that there cannot be one without the other, remains present and active in the Church: God, who spoke in the past, continues to converse with the Spouse of his beloved Son. The Holy Spirit, through whom the living voice of the Gospel rings out in the Church, and through her in the world, leads all believers to the full truth and makes the Word of Christ dwell in them in all its richness (cf. Colossians 3:16).

The Church, "the pillar and foundation of truth" (1 Timothy 3:15), faithfully guards "the faith that was once for all handed down to the holy ones" (Jude 3). She guards the memory of Christ's words. It is she who, from generation to generation, hands on the apostle's confession of faith. As a mother who teaches her children to speak and so to understand and communicate, the Church, our Mother, teaches us the *language* of faith in order to introduce us to the understanding and the *life* of faith.

Sacred Scripture and Sacred Tradition, then, are bound closely together and communicate one with the other. Both of them, flowing out from the same divine wellspring, come together, in some fashion, to form one thing and to move toward the same goal. Each of them makes present and fruitful in the Church the mystery of Christ, who promised to remain with his own "always, until the end of the age" (Matthew 28:20).

Sacred Scripture is the speech of God as it is put down in writing with the breath of the Holy Spirit. Tradition transmits, in its entirety, the Word of God that Christ entrusted to the apostles so that, enlightened by the Spirit of truth, they may faithfully preserve, expound, and spread it abroad by their preaching.

As a result, the Church, to whom the transmission and interpretation of Revelation is entrusted, does not derive her certainty about all revealed truths from the Scriptures alone. Both Scripture and Tradition must be accepted and honored with equal sentiments of devotion and reverence.

The Tradition here in question comes from the apostles and hands on what they received from Jesus' teaching and example and what they learned from the Holy Spirit. The first generation of Christians did not yet have a written New Testament, and the New Testament itself demonstrates the process of living Tradition.

Tradition, it must be noted, is to be distinguished from the various theological, disciplinary, liturgical, or devotional traditions born in the local churches over time. These are the particular forms, adapted to different places and times, in which the great Tradition is expressed. In the light of Tradition, these traditions can be retained, modified, or even abandoned under the guidance of the Church's Magisterium or teaching authority.

The diverse liturgical traditions have arisen by the very reason of the Church's mission. Churches of the same geographical and cultural area came to celebrate the mystery of Christ through particular expressions characterized by the culture: in the tradition of the "deposit of faith," in liturgical symbolism, in the organization of fraternal communion, in the theological understanding of the mysteries, and in various forms of holiness. The Church is catholic, capable of integrating into her unity, while purifying them, all the authentic riches of cultures.

The apostles entrusted the "sacred deposit" of faith (cf. 1 Timothy 6:20; 2 Timothy 1:12-14), contained in Sacred Scripture and Tradition, to the whole Church. By adhering to this heritage, the entire holy people, united to its pastors, remains always faithful to the teaching of the apostles, to the fellowship, to the breaking of bread and to the prayers. In maintaining, practicing, and professing the faith that has been handed on, there should be a remarkable harmony between the bishops and the faithful.

The task of giving an authentic interpretation of the Word of God, whether in its written form or in the form of Tradition, has been entrusted to the living, teaching office of the Church alone. Its authority in this matter is exercised in the name of Jesus Christ. This means that the task of interpretation has been entrusted to the bishops in communion with the successor of Peter, the

Bishop of Rome.

Yet, this Magisterium is not superior to the Word of God but its servant. It teaches only what has been handed on to it. At the divine command and with the help of the Holy Spirit, it listens to this devotedly, guards it with dedication, and expounds it faithfully. It draws from this single deposit of faith all that it proposes for belief as being divinely revealed.

The Christian economy, since it is the new and definitive Covenant, will never pass away. And, no new public revelation is to be expected before the glorious manifestation of our Lord Jesus Christ. Yet, even if Revelation is already complete, it has not been made completely explicit. It remains for Christian faith gradually to grasp its full significance over the course of the centuries.

Thanks to the assistance of the Holy Spirit, the understanding of both the realities and the words of the heritage of faith is able, thus, to grow in the life of the Church:

--through the contemplation and study of believers who keep all these things, reflecting on them in their hearts" (cf. Luke 2:19; 51). The tradition of Christian prayer is one of the ways in which the tradition of faith takes shape and grows, especially through the contemplation and study of believers who treasure in their hearts the events and words of the economy of salvation and through their profound grasp of the spiritual realities they experience;

--it is, in particular, theological research that deepens knowledge of revealed truth. In the work of teaching and applying Christian morality, the Church needs the dedication of pastors, the knowledge of theologians, and the contribution of all Christians and people of good will. Faith and the practice of the Gospel provide each person with an experience of life "in Christ," who enlightens and makes him or her able to evaluate the divine and human realities according to the Spirit of God (cf. 1 Corinthians 2:10-15). Thus, the Holy Spirit can use the humblest to enlighten the learned and those in the highest positions:

--from the intimate sense of spiritual realities that believers experience, the sacred Scripture "grow with the one who reads them" (St. Gregory the Great, *Homily on Ezekiel* 1, 7, 8);

--from the preaching of those who have received, along with their right of succession in the episcopate, the sure charism of truth.

It is clear, therefore, that, in the supremely wise arrangement of God, sacred Tradition, Sacred Scripture, and the Magisterium of the Church, like a three-legged stool, are so connected and associated that one of them cannot stand without the others. Working together, each in its own way, under the action of the one Holy Spirit, they all contribute effectively to the salvation of souls.

The Church and Unity

This is the sole Church of Christ that we profess in the Creed to be one, holy, catholic, and apostolic. To believe that the Church is "holy" and "catholic," and that she is "one" and "apostolic" (as the Nicene Creed adds), is inseparable from belief in God, the Father, the Son, and the Holy Spirit. In the Apostles' Creed, we profess "one Holy Church" and not to believe *in* the Church so as not to confuse God with his works and to attribute clearly to God's goodness all the gifts he has bestowed on his Church.

These four characteristics or marks, inseparably linked with one another, indicate essential features of the Church and her mission. The Church does not possess them of herself. It is Christ who, through the Holy Spirit, makes his Church one, holy, catholic, and apostolic and calls her to realize each of these qualities.

The Church is one because of her source: the highest exemplar and source of this mystery is the unity of the Trinity of Persons, of one God, the Father and the Son in the Holy Spirit.

The Church is one because of her founder: the

Word made flesh, the prince of peace, reconciled all people to God by the Cross, restoring the unity of all in one People and in one Body.

The Church is one because of her soul: it is the Holy Spirit, dwelling in those who believe and pervading and ruling over the entire Church, who brings about that wonderful communion of the faithful and joins them together so intimately in Christ that he is the principle of the Church's unity. Unity, therefore, is of the essence of the Church.

From the beginning, this one Church has been marked by a great diversity that comes from both the variety of God's gifts and the diversity of those who receive them. Within the unity of the People of God, a multiplicity of peoples and cultures is gathered together.

Among the Church's members, there are different gifts, offices, conditions, and ways of life. The very differences that the Lord has willed to put between the members of his Body serve its unity and mission.

In the Church, there is a diversity of ministry but unity of mission. To the apostles and their successors, Christ has entrusted the office of teaching, sanctifying, and governing in his Name and by his power. Christ is himself the source of ministry in the Church. He instituted the Church. He gave her authority and mission, orientation and goals.

In order to shepherd the People of God and to increase its numbers without cease, Christ the Lord set up in his Church a variety of offices that aim at the good of the whole Body. The holders of office, who are invested with a sacred power, are, in fact, dedicated to promoting the interests of their brethren so that all who belong to the People of God may attain to salvation. But, the laity, also, are made to share in the priestly, prophetic, and kingly office of Christ. They have, in the Church and in the world, their own assignment in the mission of the whole People of God.

No one, no individual and no community, can proclaim the Gospel to himself or herself: "Faith comes from what is heard" (Romans 10:17). No one can give himself or herself the mandate and the mission to proclaim the Gospel. The one sent by the Lord does not speak and act on his or her own authority but by virtue of Christ's authority, not as a member of the community but speaking to it in the Name of Christ. No one can bestow grace on himself or herself; it must be given and offered.

This fact presupposes ministers of grace, authorized and empowered by Christ. From him, they receive the mission and faculty ("the sacred power") to act in the person of Christ the Head.

The ministry, whereby Christ's emissaries do and give by God's grace what they cannot do and give by their own power, is called a "sacrament" by the Church's Tradition. Indeed, the ministry of the

Church is conferred by a special sacrament.

It belongs to the sacramental nature of ecclesial ministry that it has a collegial character. Every bishop exercises his ministry from within the Episcopal College, in communion with the bishop of Rome, the successor of St. Peter and head of the College. So also, priests exercise their ministry from within the presbyterium of the diocese, under the direction of their bishop.

As we have seen above, when Christ instituted the Twelve, he constituted them in the form of a College or permanent Assembly, at the head of which he placed Peter, chosen from among them (cf. Luke 6:13; John 21: 15-17). Just as, by the Lord's institution, St. Peter and the rest of the apostles constitute a single apostolic College, so, in like fashion, the Roman Pontiff, Peter's successor, and the bishops, the successors of the apostles, are related with and united to one another.

As we saw in Part I, the Lord made Simon alone, whom he named Peter, the "rock" of his Church. He gave him the keys of his Church and instituted him shepherd of the whole flock (cf. Matthew 16:18 & 19). Simon Peter holds the first place in the college of the Twelve; Jesus entrusted a unique mission to him.

Christ, the "living stone" (1 Peter 2:4), thus, assures his Church, built on Peter, of victory over the powers of death and hell. Because of the faith he confessed, Peter will remain the unshakeable rock of the Church. His mission will be to keep this faith from every lapse and to strengthen his brothers in it (cf. Luke 22:32).

The office of binding and loosing that was given to Peter was later also assigned to the college of apostles united to its head (John 21:15-17). This pastoral office of Peter and the other apostles belongs to the Church's very foundation and is continued by the bishops under the primacy of the Pope.

The Pope, the Bishop of Rome and Peter's successor, is the perpetual and visible source and foundation of the unity both of the bishops and of the whole company of the faithful. "For with this church, by reason of its preeminence, the whole Church, that is the faithful everywhere, must necessarily be in accord" (St. Irenaeus, *Against Heresies III, 2,* Part II).

Indeed, "from the incarnate Word's descent to us, all Christian churches everywhere have held and hold the great Church that is here [at Rome] to be their only basis and foundation since, according to the Savior's promise, the gates of hell have never prevailed against her." (St. Maximus the Confessor, *Theological Works*).

The Roman Pontiff, by reason of his office as Vicar of Christ and as pastor of the entire Church, has full, supreme, and universal power over the whole Church, the "power of the keys," from Peter and from Peter's successors, which he can always exercise unhindered.

Bishops, with priests as co-workers, have as their first task "to proclaim the Gospel to every creature" in keeping with the Lord's command (Mark 16:15). They are heralds of faith who draw new disciples to Christ. They are authentic teachers of the apostolic faith, endowed with the authority of Christ.

In order to preserve the Church in the purity of the faith handed on to the apostles, Christ, who is the Truth, willed to confer on her a share in his own infallibility. To fulfill this service, Christ endowed the Church's shepherds with the charism of infallibility in matters of faith and morals. The exercise of this charism takes several forms.

The Roman Pontiff, head of the College of bishops, enjoys this infallibility by virtue of his office when, as supreme pastor and teacher of all the faithful who confirms his brethren in the faith, proclaims, by a definitive act, a doctrine pertaining to faith or morals. The infallibility promised to the Church is also present in the body of bishops when, together with Peter's successor, they exercise the supreme Teaching Office (Magisterium), above all in an Ecumenical Council.

When the Church, through the Magisterium, proposes a doctrine for belief as being divinely revealed and as the teaching of Christ, the definitions must be adhered to with the *obedience of faith*. This infallibility extends as far as the deposit of divine Revelation itself.

Divine assistance is also given to the successors of the apostles teaching in communion with the successor of Peter and, in a particular way, to the bishop of Rome, pastor of the whole Church, when, without arriving at an infallible definition and without pronouncing it in a "definitive manner," they propose, in the exercise of the ordinary Magisterium, a teaching that leads to better understanding of Revelation in matters of faith and morals. To this ordinary teaching, the faithful are to adhere with *religious assent* that, though distinct from the assent of faith, is nonetheless an extension of it.

Finally, the bishops, as vicars and legates of Christ, govern the particular churches assigned to them by their counsels, exhortations, and example but, over and above that, by the authority and sacred power that, indeed, they ought to exercise so as to build them up in the spirit of service, which is that of their Master.

"Let all follow the bishops as Jesus Christ follows his Father and the college of presbyters as the apostles; respect the deacons as you do God's Law. Let no one do anything concerning the Church in separation from the bishop." (St. Ignatius of Antioch, *Letter To The Smyrnaeans, 8:1,* Part II)

--compiled by Patrick J. Hession from the *Catechism of the Catholic Church*

Cardinal John Henry Newman's Dilemma

Before the publication of his classic *Apologia Pro Vita Sua*, it was fashionable to espouse anti-Catholic and anti-papist sentiments in England. Newman starts his *Apologia* with an account of the beginning of his life. He was born to middle-class parents in London. At age 15, he came to Trinity College, Oxford, where he spent the next 29 years studying and teaching.

What sharply separated Newman from the Catholic Church is that Newman believed, from his youth, that "the Pope is the Antichrist." In fact, at Christmas in 1824, he preached a sermon to that effect. Newman says that he followed distinguished Protestant authorities in believing that Gregory I, around the year A.D. 600, was the first Pope who sold out to the devil, and the Council of Trent in the 16th. Century cemented the Catholic alliance with Mephistopheles. Further, Newman believed that Catholics practiced idolatry in their worship of the Virgin Mary and the saints.

During the 1830's, Newman developed his well-known *Via Media* (middle course), a sort of mid-point between Catholicism and Anglicanism.

Newman's basic argument during this point in his life was that both Catholics and Anglicans descended from the same authentic religious roots, the "primitive" Church of St. Augustine and St. Athanastasius. But, both had departed from the original wisdom, Newman believed: the Catholic Church, by "adding on" doctrines such as the Assumption of Mary into heaven, the Anglican church, for having cut itself off from the true Church through schism.

The issue for Newman, then, was *catholicity* versus *apostolicity*. This ideal religion would embody both, universal and yet legitimately descended. Newman's *Via Media*, then, was to nudge both the "errant" theologies in the direction of what he considered the true Church, one that abjured the "errors" of both Catholicism and Anglicanism while retaining their good points.

What caused Newman to abandon the *Via Media* and move headlong toward Catholicism? Why did Newman leave what he himself termed "the happiest time of my life" in order to join a controversial group of papists? The first reason was a realization of a fundamental problem at the core of Protestantism.

Protestants say that they only trust in the word of the Bible, but nowhere does the Bible ask them to do this. It is the Church Tradition that has, from the onset, directed believers to the Scripture as the inerrant word of God.

Newman's study of the ancient Church controversies, the heresies of the Monophysites and the Arians, brought him something of an epiphany about Anglicanism. Newman found, "It was difficult to [find arguments to condemn] the Popes of the 16th. Century without condemning the Popes of the 5th."

This was confirmed in Newman's Arian study. He saw that the arguments of the reviled heretics were identical in substance, and very nearly in form, to those of his current-day Protestant friends, except that his contemporaries tried to distinguish themselves from the early-Church heresies and claim a legitimate lineage back to Christ and the apostles.

Previously, Newman had regarded the choice between the Church and the Anglican churches as one between universality and antiquity. But, his study of St. Augustine, then as now a beacon that all Protestants cherish because of his emphasis on justification by faith, convinced Newman how wrong he had been.

St. Augustine was one of the prime oracles of antiquity, and yet, Newman read of his reverence for the Popes, his apparent conviction that one could not be saved outside the Catholic Church, and the passion with which he fought those who tried to revise the teachings of the Church and polarize it.

From the end of 1841, Newman's *Apologia* tells us, "I was on my deathbed as regards my membership with the Anglican church." He did not leave for four more years. But, in 1842, Newman resigned his tutorship and chaplaincy at Saint Mary's and moved to a retirement center at Littlemore. The reason was plain. Newman was not ready to become a Catholic yet, but he did not feel comfortable preaching in an Anglican church.

Gradually, Newman writes, "I came to see that the Anglican Church was formally in the wrong and that the Church of Rome was formally in the right so no valid reason could be assigned for continuing in the Anglican and no valid objections could be taken to joining the Roman." In 1843, Newman published a retraction of his previous anti-Catholic statements.

Still, one doubt persisted on Newman's mind. For years, he had defended what he calls "the dogmatic principle," or the principle of absolute truth, through the *Via Media*, and many had listened. "It is not easy, humanly speaking, to wind up an Englishman to a dogmatic level," Newman admits, and, thus, to persuade so many that the *Via Media* was preferable to theological liberalism was quite an accomplishment. But, Newman wondered "in breaking the *Via* to pieces, would not dogmatic faith be broken up altogether?"

On October 9, 1845, Father Dominic Barberi, a

missionary priest from Italy, received Newman into the Catholic Church. Newman left Oxford in 1846 and was not to visit it for at least 30 years. The next year, Newman went to Rome and was ordained a Catholic priest.

--Dinesh D'Souza, edited by Patrick J. Hession

Ministries and Offices in the First Century Church

In Acts, the Church is ruled and directed by the Spirit promised by Jesus (1:8), whose descent constitutes the beginning of her mission to the people of the whole world gathered together (2). It is the Spirit who directs every step in the expansion of the Church, who fills the ministers of the Church (4:8; 6:5; 7:55; 9:17; 11:24) as he filled the Old Testament prophets (1:16; 28:25). But, the Spirit also fills all those who belong to the Church. The manifestations of the Spirit are the signs that people are accepted into the community of believers (10:44-47; 11:17).

The Spirit is normally imparted through the ministry of the apostles (8:15-17) or other ministers (8:38; 19:6). Apostles and prophets were the foundation of the church and the receivers of divine revelation (Ephesians 2:20; 3:4 & 5; Acts 21:10).

Thus, there is also a visible authority in the Church. At the center are the apostles. As a Body, they form the link with the Christ of history and the patriarchs of the new Israel and must, therefore, be made up to the number of the Twelve, even before the coming of the Spirit. We glimpse them acting also as a College, sending their representatives (8:15), conferring authority on Stephen (6:6), accepting Paul (9:27), as well as generally bearing witness, teaching, and healing.

The only individual apostle, however, of whom any special incidents are related, is Peter. It is Peter who speaks at Pentecost. He is the first to work a miracle (3) and to suffer persecution for Christ's Name. He is the judge of Ananias and Sapphira (5). Most significantly of all, it is Peter who takes the responsibility of carrying out the vital step of accepting the first gentiles into the Church, of justifying this step before the community (10-11), and of defending the independence of gentile Christians at the Council of Jerusalem (15). It is certain that Luke regards Peter's authority as an irrefutable guarantee. But, the community itself is also seen to possess authority. They elect and present Stephen and his fellows (6:3-5) and confirm the decision of the apostles and elders at the Council of Jerusalem. (15:22).

As time goes on, we find a supplementary authority appearing in the Church, the elders. These appear first at Jerusalem (11:30), where they are later (21:18) in charge of the community under James, when the apostles have disappeared. There are elders in each community, though there is no mention of any presiding officers except James in Jerusalem. Paul established them in all the communities that he founded on his first missionary journey (14:23). It is to the elders at Ephesus that his pastoral charge is addressed. They are the "guardians of the flock," established by the Holy Spirit to guide and protect it in Paul's absence (20:28-30).

Paul was simply establishing for the Christian communities the same organization as the Jewish Communities of the Diaspora possessed; each synagogue had its own board of elders. How these elders worked together is unknown. Apart from Jerusalem, where James had some special authority (12:17), there is no sign of any institution that will later develop into the monarchical episcopate.

The *office of elder* is not mentioned until the Pastoral Epistles (1 & 2 Timothy, Titus). The Pastoral Epistles form the classical place in the New Testament for the ministry. It must be said from the outset that we should not hope to find the exact equivalent of bishop, priest, and deacon in the ministers of these epistles. But, there is clear evidence in Ignatius of Antioch (c. A.D. 109) of the monarchical episcopate, at least in some communities. The triple ministry is attested already by 1 Clement 40 (c. A.D. 95).

In Acts 20:17-28, the elders are called both priests or presbyters (presbyteroi) and overseers or bishops (episkopoi) and are said to have care of the flock. No differences in rank are apparent, but any council must have its president. *Episkopos* is the word used by the Septuagint to translate *paqid,* the president of Qumran, or words derived from this root. There are *presbyteroi*, of whom some preside, some preach and teach (1 Timothy 5:17-18) in every town (Titus 1:5). Not clearly differentiated from them but always in the singular, there is an *episkopos* (1 Timothy 3:1-7; Titus 1:7-9). Their office is somewhat similar since much of the same qualities are required for each official. It is, however, only the *episkopos* who is called "God's steward" (Titus 1:7) and who teaches.

In the light of the other documents, then, it is reasonable to conclude that a council of *presbyteroi* guided the community, one of whom presided as *episkopos*. If, as seems likely, the instructions of 1 Timothy envisage only one community, then the office of *episkopos* is not yet permanent since several elders are envisaged as filling it, with varying diligence and reward (1 Timothy 5:17). In addition, the community has *deacons*. No more can be said than that the qualities required of deacons are consonant with an office more concerned with provision and money than with teaching and directing.

Both Paul (Ephesians 3:7) and Christ himself (Romans 18:5) are described as "deacons," i.e. ministers. Stephen and his six colleagues, generally regarded as the first deacons, are never, in fact, so called. Their ministry is not much different from that of the apostles themselves. According to Acts 6:1-4, the Seven are concerned with material ministrations, but Acts does not call them deacons. They are distributors of poor relief, who, thereby, spare the Twelve from being distracted from prayer and the "ministry of the word." Elsewhere, it is clear that the Seven are full of the Spirit (6:3), work miracles 6:8), evangelize, and baptize (8:12, 38; 21:8) just as the apostles do. Therefore, it has been suggested that the Seven form a hierarchy for the Hellenist element in the community, ordained by and loosely subordinated to the Twelve.

Acts 6:6 describes the first case in the New Testament of the conferring of an office by the imposition of hands. This was common in the Old Testament (Numbers 27:23; Deuteronomy 34:9). It was a real leaning on, by which the personality of the one ordaining was poured and pressed into the ordained. Ordination by imposition of hands is the normal practice by the time of 1 Timothy 4:14 and 2 Timothy 1:16.

Of appointment of ministers we learn little. A previous examination to determine their fitness is mentioned only for deacons (1 Timothy 3:10), but this was normal practice in the Hellenistic world before the assumption of any public office. Responsibility for their appointment is laid squarely upon Timothy (1 Timothy 5:22); the people seem to play no part.

In the appointment of Paul and Barnabas as missioners by the church of Antioch (Acts 13:1-3), prophets played some part in their designation, and several people laid hands on them. In Timothy's own appointment, again prophets took part (1 Timothy 1:18), and the imposition of hands seems to have been done by the presbyters. This ceremony tells us nothing of the appointment of other ministers.

--Henry Wansbrough, A New Catholic Commentary on Holy Scripture, pages 1078 & 1079, 1210, and 1085, edited by Patrick J. Hession

Gifted Ministers

"I, then, a prisoner of for the Lord, urge you to live in a manner worthy of the call you have received, with all humility and gentleness, with patience, bearing with one another through love, striving to preserve the unity of the spirit through the bond of peace: one Body and one Spirit, as you were also called to the one hope of your call, one Lord, one faith, one baptism, one God and Father of all, who is over all and through all and in all. But, grace was given to each of us according to the measure of Christ's gift. And, he gave some as apostles, others as prophets, others as evangelists, others as pastors and teachers to equip the holy ones for the work of ministry, for building up the Body of Christ until we all attain to the unity of faith and knowledge of the Son of God, to mature manhood, to the extent of the full stature of Christ so that we may no longer be infants, tossed by waves and swept along by every wind of teaching arising from human trickery, from their cunning in the interests of deceitful scheming" (Ephesians 4:1-7, 11-14).

"Now you are Christ's Body, and individually parts of it. Some people God has designated in the Church to be, first, apostles, second, prophets, third, teachers, then, mighty deeds, then gifts of healing, assistance, administration, and varieties of tongues. Are all apostles? Are all prophets? Are all teachers? Do all work mighty deeds? Do all have gifts of healing? Do all speak in tongues? Do all interpret? Strive eagerly for the greatest spiritual gifts" (1 Corinthians 12:27-31).

"As in one body we have many parts, and all the parts do not have the same function, so we, though many, are one Body in Christ and individually parts of one another. Since we have gifts that differ according to the grace given to us, let us exercise them: if prophecy, in proportion to the faith, if ministry, in ministering, if one exhorts, in exhortation, if one contributes, with generosity, if one is over others, with diligence, if one does acts of mercy, with cheerfulness" (Romans 12:4-8).

"Living the truth in love, we should grow in every way into him who is the Head, Christ, from whom the whole Body, joined and held together by every supporting ligament, with the proper functioning of each part, brings about the Body's growth and builds itself up in love" (Ephesians 4:15 & 16).

"Allow the prophets to give thanks as much as they will. Whoever will come and teach you all the aforesaid, receive him. But, if the teacher himself turns and teaches another doctrine, do not listen to him. If it will be to the increase of righteousness and of the knowledge of the Lord, receive him as the Lord. As concerning the apostles and prophets, do according to the teaching of the gospel. Let every apostle that comes to you be received as the Lord. He should stay but one day, or two if need be, but, if he stays three days, he is a false prophet.

"Not everyone who speaks in the spirit is a prophet but only if he has the ways of the Lord. Therefore, by their ways shall be known the false prophet and the prophet. Every prophet that teaches the truth, if he or she does not do what he or she teaches, is a false prophet.

"Let everyone who 'comes in the Name of the Lord' be received. Then, when you have proved him, you will know for you can know the right hand from the left. If he wishes to live among you, being a craftsman, let him work and eat. If he doesn't have a craft, use your common sense to provide that he may live with you as a Christian, without idleness. If he is unwilling to do so, he is a 'Christ-monger.' Beware of him.

"Every prophet who wills to live among you is 'worthy of his food.' In like manner, a true teacher is also, like the laborer, 'worthy of his food.'

Bishops and deacons (are) worthy of the Lord, men who are gentle and not covetous, true men and approved. They also minister to you the ministry of the prophets and teachers. Therefore, do not despise them for they are to be honored by you with the prophets and teachers" (The Didache, or Teaching of the Twelve Apostles (c 100) 11, 12, 15).

Apostles in the Church

The institution of the episcopate, as it developed in the first century and continues in the Church, is to be understood only in relation to the institution of the apostles by Christ. Examination of the texts in the New Testament permits one to make the following observations:

Apostles are called to the *service of the whole Church*, a service that finds its most perfect example in Christ, who came not to be served but to serve (Mark 10:42-45; Matthew 20:25-28).

According to Matthew 28:19 & 20, their mission is to teach all people, to sanctify them by the sacraments, and to bring the faithful to obey the commands of the Lord.

In order to accomplish this mission, the apostles receive a special gift of the Holy Spirit (John 20:21-23; Acts 1:8; 2:2-5).

Each of the apostles receives this mission and this gift in union with the other apostles. Together they form a whole, a well-defined Body to which the New Testament often applies the expression *The Twelve* (Mark 3:14-16, etc.). It is to this group that Matthias is admitted to become *with them* a witness of the Resurrection (Acts 1:26).

To this group, the unity of which is so manifest, one can apply the title "College," provided that one does not take it to mean that all the members of it are equal. Peter occupies a special place and is endowed with a higher authority, which no one contests, founded as it is on the words of Christ himself (Matthew 16:16ff; Luke 22:31ff).

The office of the apostles was not to cease with them. They chose helpers in their tasks of preaching and governing the communities (cf. Philippians 2:25; Colossians 4:11). These helpers shared the apostles' authority (cf. Acts 20:28). The faithful are to recognize them as their rulers (cf. Hebrews 13:7, 13, 24).

It is not always possible to distinguish between "elders" or "presbyters" (Acts 11:30; 14:23) and "bishops" (Philippians 1:1; Acts 20:28, etc.).

The fellow-workers of the apostles are warned not to try to lord it over the faithful (1 Peter 5:3). Their office, like that of the apostles, is a ministry, a service for the good of the community.

From the beginning, in appointing collaborators, they used a liturgical rite consisting of prayer and the laying on of hands, signifying the gift of a special grace or charism in view of the task to be fulfilled. A similar rite was used for the appointment of the first deacons (Acts 6:6) and of the presbyters in the course of the journeys of St Paul (Acts 14:28). In the case of Timothy (1 Timothy 4:4; 2 Timothy 1:6), the laying on of hands conferred a special spiritual gift, that of "power, love, and self-control," like that which St. Paul himself was conscious of having received (Timothy 1:7, 11).

--Joseph Lecuyer, Encyclopedia of Theology, pages 147 & 148, edited by Patrick J. Hession

Apostles in the Church - Further Reflections

The Institution of the Twelve

Most exegetes seem to agree that, during his public life, Christ gathered around him a more or less stable group of disciples, according to the rabbinical usage, "to be with him" (Mark 3:13 & 14). Very early, probably during the lifetime of Christ, they were named "The Twelve," a symbolic title that envisioned the origins (the patriarchs) and the end of time (Matthew 19:23; Luke 22:28-30) and, hence, also signified the new people of God (the twelve tribes).

They were Christ's helpers in the preaching of the kingdom (Mark 6:7-13; Luke 9:1-6). Their mission was confirmed after the Resurrection and then became universal, as is very clear in Matthew, where stress had been laid on the fact that Christ's own mission was confined to the chosen people (cf. Matthew 28:16-20). Their mission was also unique in a certain sense since they were the privileged witnesses of the life, death, and Resurrection of the Lord (cf. Luke 24:48 & 49; Acts 1:4-11).

The Mission of the Twelve

The synoptic gospels attribute a special mission to the Twelve that cannot, however, be neatly distinguished from the mission of others who believed in Christ. Thus, Matthew, in the discourse edited by the evangelist and addressed to the Twelve (Matthew 9:35-11:1), incorporates a number of sayings that, in a different editorial context (e.g. Matthew 18, context of the Christian Community) refers to all the faithful.

One might also point to the passage proper to Luke, that of the 70 or 72 disciples (cf. Luke 10:1-24), a text which is difficult to interpret but which Luke has undoubtedly placed at one of the high-points of his gospel, between the counsels given to the Twelve (cf. Luke 9:46-62) and the "hymn of jubilation" (cf. Luke 10:21-24).

Exegetes agree, in general, that the number 70 (or 72 - 6x12) implies an *institutional* authority (cf. the 70 "elders" of Moses, Exodus 24:1; Numbers 11: 16, the symbol and tradition persisting to the time of Christ) or a *universal* authority (the world has 70 people groups or 70 languages).

Luke may have been wishing to justify the government of the Pauline Churches by *episcopoi-presbyteri*, or rather, as seems more probable, he was thinking of the universal apostolic mission of the people of God. Then, the famous text, "He who hears you hears me," which is applied so frequently to the Episcopal Magisterium, would refer in this context to the prophetic testimony of all the faithful before the world.

The same ambivalence recurs in the word by which the synoptics mainly define the ministry of the Twelve, the *diakonia*. Christ's mission is a *diakonia* (e.g. Luke 22:26f, where the normal and original meaning of the word is still recognizable: to serve at table). So, too, is the mission of all the faithful since they are "servants of God and of men," inspired by charity (e.g. Matthew 23:11f; John 12:25f). But, the ministry of the Twelve is described with a special insistence as "service" (Mark 9:35; 10:43f; Matthew 20:26-28).

The special mission of the Twelve is to share in the mission given to Christ by the Father: the preaching of the kingdom. This is asserted by the three synoptics (Mark 9:32-42; Matthew 10:10-42; Luke 9:46-50). If Luke 10:1-24 envisages, in fact, the *episcopi-presbyteri* of the Pauline Churches, the same assertion is found in 10:16, in a form adapted to Greek readers. John repeats it in another form at the end of his gospel (John 20:19-23), where this mission is explicitly linked with the gift of the Holy Spirit in view of the remission of sins, equivalent to the conversion of heart preached in the synoptics in view of the kingdom.

The same notion of participation in the mission of Christ seems to be expressed in concrete symbolism in the three images of the servant or child (the Aramaic *talia* can mean both), shepherd, and rock.

The rabbis called themselves the "great" and their disciples the "little ones" or the "children." Thus, when sharing in the mission of the "Servant of God," the Twelve are compared to "children" or "little ones." Christ shows them a child, which is a parable in action. Throughout this context, it is notable that Christ contrasts the exercise of the Twelve's authority with that of the great ones of this world and of the rabbis but does not speak of that of the priests of Judaism.

Christ is the good shepherd. Peter (John 21:15-18), the Twelve (Matthew 9:35-38), and the other ministers (1 Peter 5:2) are also shepherds. Christ is, after Yahweh, the rock of Israel. So, too, Peter is called Rock (Matthew 16:13-20), and the Twelve are the "columns" or the "foundation" (Ephesians 2:20; Galatians 2:9; Revelation 21:14). Christ is to suffer for the sake of the kingdom. So, too, the disciples. Christ is the prophet, and they, too, are to preach the kingdom. Christ is the new Moses, and the disciples are to be his "seventy elders" (according to a probable interpretation of Luke 10:1-24).

The Apostolate

The rethinking of the original fact of the Twelve as envoys of Christ in terms of the new notion of "apostle" is probably due to Paul and Luke. In the strict sense of the term, an apostle is a witness of the life and death of Christ, by virtue of the gift of the Spirit by which he receives a universal mission (Acts 1:21ff). This unique role is extended to Matthias (Acts 1:24ff), to Paul, and to James, the brother of the Lord, who did not, apparently, belong to the college of the Twelve. For such an extension, it seems that Paul and Luke presuppose a direct intervention by God (through the casting of lots) or a vision of the risen Christ. Later on, the word apostle is used in a wider sense, which seems to be based simply on the notion of universal preaching. This is an analogous and subsidiary use of the title.

The Origin of the Ecclesiastical Hierarchy

On the historical plane, it seems impossible ever to arrive at definitive conclusions as to the concrete origin of the ecclesiastical ministry as we now know it. No one doubts the importance of the Twelve. But, soon other "apostles" were added, whose authenticity seems to have been recognized by all for reasons that mostly remain unknown to us. Others were then joined to these, with an authority at the beginning very like that of the apostles, the "prophets and teachers" (1 Corinthians 12:28; Acts 13:1; 15:22; Ephesians

2:20, 3:5, 4:11). They soon yielded their authority to others. Their successors seem to have had an authority based, rather, on an *institution* than on a *charism*, though the distinction should not be overworked.

There are "superiors" (cf. 1 Thessalonians 5:12) in a position of authority (cf. Romans 12:8), sometimes called "guides" (1 Corinthians 12:28; cf. Acts 27:11; Revelation 18:17) or "pastors" (1 Corinthians 12:28; Ephesians 4:11). Paul only mentions the *episcopoi* (bishops, Philippians 1:1) once before the "deacons." This title is probably of Hellenistic origin (cf. Acts 20:28, where the office is compared to that of a shepherd).

At an early stage, the apostles at Jerusalem called in the "Seven" as helpers (cf. Acts 6:1-6). These are traditionally the first deacons. However they seem to have been the first type of "presbyters" or elders, modeled on the Jewish institution. These elders formed a governing body, a type of religious authority fairly widespread in the Jewish diaspora, to which a parallel may be found at Qumran. The elders, as such, are first mentioned at Jerusalem (Acts 11:30, 15:2-23, 16:4, 21:18, 22:15), then, later, in other places (Acts 14:23, 20:17-35; James 5:14; 1 Peter 5:1, 5). Later, still, they are under the authority of a disciple of the Apostle Paul (1 Timothy 3:5, 5:17, 19, 22; Titus 1:5).

These are scattered and fairly disparate indications. With only this to go on, the historian can hardly venture very far. It is fairly clear, nevertheless, that the apostles claimed, at a very early stage, the right to call on "helpers" whose responsibilities are not very well defined, while reserving to themselves the general direction of the Churches that they had founded.

This evidence does not permit us to affirm that the hierarchy of orders, i.e. monarchical bishop, college of elders, and deacons, was of divine institution in the strict sense, or even an institution of the apostolic Church, considered as a norm for later Churches.

Vatican II undoubtedly affirmed that the bishop is given the fullness of the priesthood as member of the Episcopal college by the fact of his ordination, and that the priest is ordained as "helper" of the bishop. But, as we see it, the Council did not decide whether the matter in question was a dogmatic definition of a revealed reality or an act of "the ecclesiastical economy." An ancient controversy, which had gone on until the time of the Council, was, thus, closed in fact but not by law.

Laying On Of Hands

Laying on of hands was a fairly widespread rite in Judaism. In Numbers 8:5-11, the whole tribe of

Levi is set apart for the service of the covenant by the imposition of hands, that of the whole people. The "priestly" strand of the Pentateuch speaks of Moses having laid his hands upon Joshua, whereby Joshua was filled with Moses' spirit of wisdom (cf. Deuteronomy 34:8) or invested with some of his authority or dignity (cf. Numbers 27:15-20).

At a certain date, the scribes or doctors of the law, the heirs of the authority of Moses, must have adopted this collegial rite (cf. Numbers 27:22) in order to transfer their authority to their disciples. This rite was juridical but had also a quasi-sacramental character, since the disciple received, in this way, the "spirit of Moses."

The question has been raised as to whether the rabbis' envoys were confirmed in their most specific mission by the laying on of hands. The New Testament shows that Christ, and later the apostles and the "Seven," used this symbolic gesture as a sign of blessing and healing. The rite was employed very early, it seems, for the transmission of the "gifts of the Spirit."

Laying on of hands is mentioned in a number of New Testament texts with reference to the handing on of a mission in the apostolic Church. It is still debated whether Acts 13:1-3, 6:1-6, 14:22, 20 deal with truly priestly ordination. There is hardly room for doubt about 1 Timothy 4:14 and 2 Timothy 1:6 when taken together, and 1 Timothy

5:22 and Titus 1:5 may refer to an ordination.

The *rite* cannot be identified with sufficient probability until near A.D. 200. It may, therefore, be presumed that the laying on of hands is not a "substantial" element of the sacramental rite but a rite instituted by the Church.

--Piet Fransen, Encyclopedia of Theology, pages 1125-1130, edited by Patrick J. Hession

The episcopal order and the presbyteral order are based on two different ways of being Jesus' representative. In the four Gospels, the apostle is one of a College, working solely within Israel as a representative of the earthly Jesus. This Jewish-Christian, collegiate apostolate continues in the council of presbyters that we find in the local Christian community of the period of Luke's Gospel (transposed into Acts), in James, 1 Peter, Titus, 1 Timothy, and Revelation.

Contrasted with it, we have the Pauline concept of apostleship, which 2 Corinthians 8:23 shows must have prevailed in other gentile churches as well. Here, the risen Lord is represented by a single apostle and later by a single *episkopos* or overseer. There is no presbyter.

We may gather from 1 Peter 2:15 that the office is primarily one of *juridical supervision*, whereas the parallel shepherding of the flock *positively leads them to salvation*. Thus, the two functions of the office of *episkopos* are conveyed by combining the two terms.

The oldest text is Philippians 1:1, according to which there are still several *episkopoi* in the local community who have supervisory duties in the Church (see Titus 1:6ff; 1 Timothy 3:4 & 5). On the other hand, we are well on the way to the monarchical episcopate with Timothy's mission as Paul's representative.

As the apostles disappeared, representatives of this kind gather the episcopal duties into the hands of one individual. Thus, the local character and the duties of the office of *episkopos* derive from the collective episcopate, whereas its monarchical character derives from the apostolic office.

If we compare the theological concept of an apostle in 2 Corinthians with 1 Peter, we see the theological relevance of the monarchical element. According to 2 Corinthians, there can be only one apostle for the community because he alone represents and communicates with the one Lord Jesus Christ in a community of suffering and labor in the domain that is his responsibility.

1 Peter shows how the idea of the highest local authority as an image of Christ also colors the concept of the *episkopos*: Christ is *the episkopos* of the community (2:25) and its supreme shepherd (5:4).

The rulers of the community are presbyters (5:1), but their work too is *episkopos*, parallel to Christ's "shepherding" the flock. So, the presbyters' episcopal work parallels that of Christ the *episkopos*.

Here, the presbyters represent the glorified Lord, and he is pictured in their image. Several presbyters exercise the function of the supreme shepherd. In this way, 1 Peter combines the idea of an *episkopos* with *presbyteral order*. The monarchical episcopate arises from the image of Christ the one *episkopos*, blended with the Pauline idea of one apostle in each community.

Thus, the germ of the monarchical episcopate is found in the Hellenistic area that Paul evangelized, in the mission of Timothy, in 1 Peter, in 1 & 2 Timothy, and in Titus. On the other hand, by way of contrast with the synagogue, the Law, and traditional Jewish thought, Paul had no trace of presbyteral order in his communities, though that order soon penetrated his communities. By the time Acts was written, the churches in Lyconia and Pisidia had elders or presbyters.

Acts and the Letters to Timothy and Titus show us the blending of Hellenistic episcopal order with Jewish presbyteral order. In Acts 20, the presbyters (19) are called *episkopoi* (28). Possession of the Holy Spirit is the decisive criterion of their vocation and authority. We may not suppose from Acts 1:20 that the episcopate is, in itself, equivalent to the apostolate since *overseer* in this text is taken from Psalm 108:8.

Thus, the language of Acts shows that the word *episkopos* or overseer was still taken in the general sense of ruling the community and could, therefore, be applied to a presbyteral system as well.

Acts 6:3 stipulates that they be men of good standing and full of the Holy Spirit and wisdom before the apostles appointed them to their task. The apostles then prayed and laid their hands on them, thereby delegating their authority to them.

Titus 1:6-9 and 1 Timothy 3:1-13 belong to the same literary genre as Acts 20:18-38, the ideal *episkopos*. According to 1 Timothy 3:1, *episkopos* is a permanent office to which one may aspire. The qualities necessary in the candidate are described, not the duties of the office. We have, here, a basically presbyteral system crowned by episcopal order.

In 1 Timothy 5:17, those presbyters who preside well and who labor in preaching and teaching are obviously the *episkopoi*, who are worthy of double honor. They underlay the development that underlies the pre-eminence of the episcopate.

According to Titus 1:5-9, Titus is to appoint elders in Crete, just as Paul himself had done (Acts

14:23), but, in verse 7, they are also called *episkopoi*. 1 Timothy 3:2 and Titus 1:7, however, already speak of the *episkopos* or bishop in the singular. Even if this is a merely generic singular, the duties that Timothy and Titus had with regard to several communities soon pass to the individual *episkopos* so that, by the end of the first century, a single *episkopos* takes over in each local church.

--Klaus Berger, Encyclopedia of Theology, pages 142-144, edited by Patrick J. Hession

Prophets in the Church

In spite of a certain possible fluidity of roles and an actual identification at times, the prophet is different from the priest, who is the minister of divine worship. The prophet always comes forward with a new message. He or she has to produce his or her own credentials. His or her task cannot be, strictly speaking, institutionalized. Hence, the *uniqueness* of his or her vocation is what is of the *essence* of the prophet.

The prophet is the envoy of God. He or she is always, to some extent, the religious revolutionary, and, since religion and society form a unity, he or she is often the critic of society, speaking in the Name of God. Thus, the prophet proclaims a message that makes demands and does not confine himself or herself to truths that become clearly expressed or presented or easy to understand as they are set forth.

The prophet is the "bearer of revelation." He or she claims to be the envoy sent directly by God, with a primary or fundamental relationship to the Word of God. He or she is convinced that what he or she proclaims is the word of God himself. The prophet experiences himself or herself as the instrument not of a mysterious power but of a personal, "living" God who freely reveals himself.

The message the prophet brings is not really meant for the prophet alone. It is primarily for others, for those to whom he or she is sent with a mandate. Hence, the actual nature of any given prophet must be seen as intrinsically connected with his or her message, with his or her "concept of God."

The "word" is essential to the prophet and to his or her task. Thus, it is not a merely neutral record but a criticism of religion and society, an interpretation of historical events, and, indeed, as such an intrinsic or inherent element of these events, giving them their real depth and truth and allowing them to exert their full force.

The prophet may, but does not necessarily, make predictions, in the sense of an oracle or clairvoyant. Nonetheless, since he or she creates a new and forward-looking situation in the history of salvation by his or her criticism of society, the prophet is essentially associated with promises and the future.

The prophet will nearly always be the leader and organizer of religious and social changes. He or she "institutionalizes" his or her message in a strange, dangerous, but necessary paradox that conflicts with his or her own nature.

To sum up: a prophet, where the word does not merely mean the prophetic office, may be said to exist wherever a religious society accepts, on principle, the possibility of a prophet, where the coming of a new prophet is reckoned with, where prophetic criticism of traditional and institutionalized religion, of "a Church," is not ruled out from the start as irreligious, where religion is understood as much in the light of its future as of its past, and where prophetic criticism is acknowledged to be an essential element of religion itself.

Dogmatic Principles:

The prophet is of the essence of a religion that is convinced that it is established by a historical revelation given in words. Hence, the prophet is essential to the history of the Old and New Testament salvation.

The phenomenon of prophecy must occur again and again in this general history of revelation. This does not mean that there cannot be simply "false prophets" who speak only in their own name. It must also be considered that the translation into words of the general revelation, which is there with grace, and its realization in action, may be partially defective or may be relevant only within certain areas and certain periods.

Nonetheless, the prophets, as divine envoys in the Old and New Testaments, have an easily perceived historical connection, acknowledged as legitimate, with Jesus Christ. They are his acknowledged "precursors," while Jesus Christ is the vehicle of the pure and ultimately unsurpassable revelation of God, present in time as event and in his words as going to constitute this event.

If mysticism, in the full sense, is not experience of one's own "spiritual or supernatural" inwardness but the experience of grace, revelatory in character, there is no absolute opposition between mystical and prophetic experience.

Jesus Christ is *the* great prophet, the absolute bringer of salvation. This does not mean that prophecy has simply ceased. But, the only true prophets are those who strive to uphold his message in its purity, attest that message, and make it relevant to their day.

The charisms, or spiritual gifts of the Spirit, are of the essence of the Church, in spite of and throughout all its institutions. Of their nature, the spontaneous charisms that work in and for the Church are prophetic. This charismatic prophecy in the Church helps to make the message of Jesus new, relevant, and actual in each changing age.

It does not matter whether the representatives of this charismatic prophecy in the Church, the authors of religious renewal, the critics of the Church and society of their day, the discoverers of new tasks for the Church and the faithful, are called prophets or are given other names. If such people do not merely reaffirm general principles and apply them to new cases but display in their message something creative and unpredictable, with the force of historical turning points so that they are legitimate and effective in the Church, we may say that the Church has had a "major" or "minor" prophet.

The "discernment of spirits," by the defense of genuine prophecy against a conservative establishment or by the unmasking of false prophecy in the Church, can itself be a prophetic mission.

In the light of the prophetic element in the Church, the official priesthood must be subjected to a reappraisal. The priest is essentially the preacher of the Word, the prophet, and not just an administrative officer in a religious society. The priesthood combines the both the prophetic and the sacramental elements.

--Karl Rahner, Encyclopedia of Theology, pages 1286-1289, edited by Patrick J. Hession

Baptism: A Command and a Gift

Introduction

For the early Christians, Baptism was the conscious and blessed beginning of the Christian life, a new birth and re-birth in the image of Christ, accomplished by bathing in water while a few words were uttered. With the simplicity of a divine act, "the washing of water with the word" (Ephesians 5:26) brought about something incredibly magnificent, the life of eternity (cf. Tertullian *Concerning Baptism* 1-2). For the Christian of today, Baptism is still the entrance to all the sacraments, the gate to Christian life, and, hence, to the eternal life that is its ultimate consequence.

Baptism blots out original sin and all personal sins, makes Christians partakers in the divine nature through grace, gives them adoption as sons and daughters, and entitles them to the reception of the other sacraments and to the active sharing in the priestly adoration of the Church.

Words of the Lord

How the apostolic preaching interpreted "washing of water with the word of life" is plain to see in the New Testament. It is intimately bound up with the command of the risen Christ: "Go, therefore, and make disciples of all nations, baptizing them in the name of the Father, and of the Son, and of the Holy Spirit, teaching them to observe all that I have commanded you" (Matthew 28:19 & 20a).

These words certainly record the will of the glorified Christ to institute the sacrament of Baptism, though the Trinitarian formula may be an echo of apostolic practice.

The inner meaning of Baptism is intimated by the mysterious images our Lord uses in his conversation with Nicodemus (John 3:1-10). These, of course, are fully intelligible only to one who has experienced Christian baptism. At any rate, the reception of baptism is regarded from the beginning as the foundation of all discipleship and Christian life (Acts 2:37-41). After the descent of the Holy Spirit at the first Pentecost, the apostles looked upon baptism as a rite already hallowed by tradition and administered it as such.

Earlier Analogies

Attempts to show that Baptism was borrowed from the religions of the Greek world have been fruitless, but the practice is certainly foreshadowed in the Old Testament.

The Old Testament frequently mentions practices analogous to baptism, which took the form of washings; among other texts, see Exodus 40:12; Leviticus 8:6, 13:6, 14:4-9, 16:4, 24; Ezekiel 36:25. In the time of Christ, such "baptisms" or washings were much in use, e.g. Mark 7:2-4. Jewish sects like the Essenes made much of them, Josephus, *Jewish War* 2, 117-161, and they were a special feature of the Qumran community,1 QS, 6, 16f; 3, 4-9.

It is easier to understand the "baptism of John" against this background, although he contributed important new features: as an emissary of God, he baptized *others* to call them to repentance in preparation for the nobler baptism to come. Jesus' disciples baptized during his lifetime in an obviously similar manner (John 4:1-3).

Apostolic Practice

After the glorification of the Lord, the apostles administered the traditional rite in a new way and with a new importance. They now baptized in the Name of Jesus, that is, in accordance with the gospel in the Name of Jesus, assigning people to him, invoking his Name over the candidate. Finally, a further development, they baptized in the name of the Father, Son, and Holy Spirit. The continuity of usage emerges in Acts 18:25 & 26 and 19:2-6, where the transition to the new form is indicated.

The washing with water and the word is the climax of a whole process: penance and faith are perfected in baptism. With this procedure, because it intimately unites one with Christ, come salvation, the remission of sins, and the gift of the Holy Spirit. Christ is the *light* that shines in Baptism, the *life* that it bestows, the *truth* that the baptized person confess and to which he or she pledges his or her loyalty, the *source* from which flow the rivers of living water, the *water* and the *blood* from the open wound in his side. They wash away all the guilt of a person's sins.

Deeper Insights

These relatively sparse data from the synoptic gospels, from Acts, and, not least, from the fourth gospel, when full justice is done to the intentions underlying its composition, are admirably expounded in other books of the New Testament, especially in St. Paul, 1 John, and 1 Peter. These books work out a theology of the washing of water with the word as a unique personal and sacramental act that confers "being-in-Christ," which is the sum of Christian existence. "You were buried with him in baptism, in which you were also raised with him through faith in the working of God, who raised him from the dead" (Colossians 2:12).

Fruitful controversy in recent years has again brought these results to the foreground. Passing over minor obscurities and differences of interpretation, this article is concerned simply with what was arrived at in common as part of the faith.

The essential thing, then, is that, by Baptism, when we were dead through our transgressions and sins, God, who is rich in mercy, because of the great love he had for us, brought us to life with Christ, raised us up with him, and seated us with him in the heavens in Christ Jesus (cf. Ephesians 2:1, 4-6).

For all its noble simplicity, the rite of initiation through the washing of water with the word so that we may gain salvation by the forgiveness of sins and the gift of the Holy Spirit conveys several truths.

First of all, Baptism is the culmination of a person's personal encounter with God in Christ, of his or her personal response to the appeal of God's word. "Those who accepted his message were baptized" (Acts 2:41) and responded to the good news Jesus brings: "Yes, I believe that Jesus Christ is the Son of God" (Acts 8:37, the Western reading).

Baptism bodies forth the faith that is the fundamental way of our living in Christ. Without faith, it would be a lifeless outward show. But, it is more than a "symbolic" expression of active faith.

The washing by water in the word is real access to Christ and his redemption. It is "being baptized into his death." It is dying with him and rising with him, truly sharing his sufferings so that, becoming like him in his death, we may attain the resurrection from the dead (cf. Philippians 3:10f.).

Another important aspect of Baptism is that of purification. Washing of water with the word cleanses the Church (Ephesians 5:26). As this pure water sprinkles the body, it cleanses our hearts from an evil conscience (cf. Hebrews 10:22). Sharing in Christ's death and being purified in the sacred waters that flow forth from him brings about fellowship with the living Christ, a new life. One is a new creation, enjoying, even now, a share in his Resurrection that will be perfected in the future, when the Lord returns.

All this is reality, but the Christian's faith must grasp and affirm its fullness in advance, ponder the consequences, and accept them in the serious constancy of a truly Christian life. "Consequently, you, too, must think of yourselves as [being] dead to sin and living for God in Christ Jesus" (Romans 6:11).

Baptism, then, must produce the whole breadth and depth of a life rooted and grounded in Christ (cf. Ephesians 3:16-19). In Romans 6:12-14, the apostle forcefully points out the practical ethical consequences of Baptism. What is demanded of those who are baptized is nothing less than a thoroughgoing conversion. Baptism has given them a completely new being, and they must shape their lives accordingly.

The early Church took this passage from the "indicative" to the "imperative" in Baptism very seriously: "it is impossible to restore again to repentance those who have once been enlightened (in Baptism), who have tasted the heavenly gift, have become partakers of the Holy Spirit, and have tasted the goodness of the Word of God and the powers of the age to come, if they, then, commit apostasy" (Hebrews 6:4-6). This shows what weight was attached to the obligations imposed by Baptism at that time.

Controversy on Baptism by Heretics

Practical necessities drew attention to the truth that Baptism cannot be repeated. Controversy arose about Baptism conferred by schismatics and, especially, heretics.

Donatism, a schism rather than a heresy, raised the question whether the validity of the sacraments, as distinct from their effectiveness, depended on the worthiness of the minister or recipient. St.

Augustine gives the classic statement of the objectivity of the sacraments: "in the matter of Baptism, we must consider not who he is that gives it but what it is that he gives; not who he is that receives but what it is that he receives" (*Concerning Baptism,* iv. 16).

This principle underlies the theology of Baptism that St. Augustine worked out against the heretics of his own time. Augustine reaffirms that, since Christ, the author and possessor of Baptism, is its real minister, the sacrament is valid, even when administered by a heretic. The heretic, too, confers the Church's baptism, the Baptism of Christ, "which is always holy of its own nature and, therefore, does not belong to those who separate themselves but to that communion from which they separate" (*Concerning Baptism* I, 12, 19).

Later, he laid even more stress on the objective nature of the sacrament. Unless a person is in sacramental communication with Christ's redemptive act, fundamentally through Baptism and, then, through the Eucharist, "he or she cannot reach the kingdom of God nor gain salvation and eternal life."

On the other hand, Augustine never ceased to inveigh against a mechanical conception of the sacraments. Without faith, there can be no sacrament at all. Every sacrament embodies a personal act of faith, at least on the part of the

Church. It is a sacrament of this faith, a holy sign of belief in Christ and his salvation. Furthermore, though valid of itself, without love it remains barren.

Eventually, this Roman view prevailed. By defending a primacy of the official and sacramental element, independent of the personal holiness of the minister, even if he belongs to a body that is not the true Church, Rome vindicated the primacy of God's power, which is decisively exercised in Baptism regardless of human limitations. However, its *fruitfulness* depends on the dispositions of the recipient, his or her faith and love.

Such considerations finally brought it home to Christians that Baptism, conferred in the proper form, in the power of Christ who is its real minister, is and remains valid because of the sustaining faith that gives access to Christ. Here are the foundations for the later doctrine that Baptism imprints an indelible character on the soul. Once baptized, a Christian can never again be a non-Christian in character, though he or she may act otherwise through apostasy. This is what the writer of Hebrews was referring to.

It is, therefore, not correct, as some Fundamentalists and Evangelicals teach, to say that water baptism doesn't "do anything" itself, that it is simply one's public profession of the decision to follow Christ in obedience, although this is critical, as we have seen. Baptism is that sacred action of Christ himself whereby his redemption, death, and resurrection are given to us here and now, a gift, if you will, initiating us into Christian life by a concrete, tangible, symbolic confession of the faith so that we may be made conformable to the crucified and risen Lord.

What once happened to Christ now happens to us in Baptism so that we may be reborn to a new life. The Holy Spirit, sent by the risen Lord who sits at the right hand of the Father, fills and consecrates the water so that this sensible element may wash us immaculate and clothe us in splendor.

The Church Fathers from Tertullian on call this "washing of water with the word" a *sacramentum* or *mysterium*, a term they also use for other sacred acts. By the 3rd. or 4th. Century at the latest, the word had permanently acquired this technical sense.

Baptism is a sacrament, an initiation that involves swearing fidelity in the service of Christ (like the oath of allegiance, the sacramentum of the Roman soldier). But since *sacramentum* also took on the fuller force of *mysterium*, it was a sacred act that communicated symbolically what it represented and molded the believer to its likeness. As image of the death and resurrection of Christ, the mystery made the believer participate in the Passover of Christ from death to life.

Parallel to this very Pauline theology of baptism into the death of Christ, another conception looms even larger, the impregnation of the baptismal water with the sanctifying power of Christ's spirit.

Baptism produces its wonderful effects by the might of the crucified and risen Lord. He fills the water with the power of his Holy Spirit and makes it fruitful so that it may beget his new life in the Church. Thus, the writer exclaims, "This prefigured Baptism, which saves you now. It is not a removal of dirt from the body but an appeal to God for a clear conscience, through the Resurrection of Jesus Christ, who has gone into heaven and is at the right hand of God" (1 Peter 3:21 & 22a).

Infant Baptism

The baptism of adults is presupposed throughout the New Testament and the early Christian period. As yet, we find no references to the baptism of infants and young children. But, this is no proof that the practice was unknown.

The parallel between Baptism and circumcision, as a rite of initiation and entrance into the community of God's chosen people, would not have been lost on the apostles and early Christians who came out of a Jewish background. In any case, infant baptism developed naturally out of the entirely different circumstances in which Christianity found itself. It was thought fitting to receive children into the fellowship of Christ and the Church, but no special rite of infant baptism was ever devised.

In the early days, the baptism of children was something almost "incidental," a sort of appendage to the baptism of adults, which was always the main concern. Child baptism, however, became the normal practice from about the 4th. or 5th. Century on. Basically, nothing changed so that, even today, through the intermediary of their godparents, infants are treated at their baptism as if they were adults: they renounce Satan, confess the faith, and state that they wish to be baptized.

To pretend that the infant is a responsible partner is forcing matters. Our keener sense of authenticity demands that the child be treated as such, regarded as a "partner" only within his or her limitations.

We must state what really happens: here is are human beings on whom God is pleased to bestow salvation in Christ through the intermediary of the Church, his Body, giving the Church, the parents, and the sponsors the duty of bringing them to the point where they can freely affirm the saving grace they have been given and, from that point on, preserve it for themselves.

Infant baptism, thus, exists in its own right and has its own claims to our appreciation. The problems it raises have much exercised Protestant theologians. But, the fact that faith communities, including the Reformed, accept infant baptism in practice shows that they take a realistic view of Baptism and see it as something objective.

It is precisely Protestant exegetes, Church historians, and experts in comparative religion who now acknowledge the realism of the ancient Christian sacramental idea. They often emphasize "that St. Paul ascribes a 'real mystical action' to baptism that makes of the sinner a person freed from sin, who is bound, in a mysterious way, with the death and Resurrection of Christ" (Neunheuser, following M. J. Lagrange).

Thus, theologians must now stress the following points:

1. The event of Baptism is a sacred mystery. It is a sacrament that communicates grace, but it is no less a highly personal act on the part of the adult convert. As a mystery, Baptism is an act of initiation, an introduction to truly Christian life, whereby the redemptive death of Christ that happened but once in history is made present in the shape of a visible rite. The person who is baptized can die with and like Christ and rise again with him to the new life that is being-in-Christ-Jesus, in the hope of one day attaining the full glory of the resurrection.

2. If we consider the outward sign as an ablution,

then Baptism is seen to be the cleansing of sinful man in the precious Blood of the Lamb of God by the water that flowed from the open side of the Crucified Savior.

The baptismal water is the instrument Christ uses to bring about this redemptive purification: filled with the power of the Holy Spirit, on the invocation of God's Name, it purges of all sin and awakens one to the new life of those "born again of water and Spirit" (John 3:5).

The door to the kingdom of God is opened in Baptism, even for an infant. As fellowship with Christ in his crucifixion, death, and risen life, or as instrument in the hands of the Redeemer to cleanse and give grace and life, Baptism remains a sovereign act of God's omnipotence, applying Christ's redemption to the sinner out of mercy and prevenient love, without any merit on our part, and demanding, from that point on, a life of obedience to God.

3. Nothing at all in this sacramental action savors of magic. Magic, indeed, is fatal to all true religion. If the action that proceeds from faith and is achieved in baptism is unfailingly efficacious, that is simply evidence of the power of God who, of his own free grace, has willed this way of salvation appropriate to the basic event which is the incarnation of the Word, appropriate as well, therefore, to the double structure of people. Baptism proclaims the utter sufficiency of the

redemption that Christ wrought once and for all in history and that takes effect now in the sacrament.

Obligations of Baptism

Baptism imposes obligations in keeping with the spiritual nature of human beings. It gives the infant or child all it can bear: to be a child of God, freed from the burden of original sin, of the wrath of God. But, by this very fact, the infant or child has a duty, when he or she reaches the estate of a responsible person, of freely confessing the reality of his or her Baptism by faith and love and shaping his or her life accordingly, in the hope of preserving that grace until its consummation in eternity. Otherwise, Baptism would fail to achieve its real and ultimate effect.

But, Baptism addresses adult converts directly. Unless they approache the sacrament in the dispositions that become a responsible person, yields the assent of their faith, resolutely turns their back on sin, and freely commit themselves to Christ crucified and risen, the baptism remains barren, even though it may be correctly administered and even though it truly gives converts that first contact with Christ that mark them forever as Christ's possession so that, whatever their present deficiencies, they can, at any time, turn repentant to the Lord and giver of true life.

Baptism is living fellowship with Christ, the

inauguration of that New Testament life that is inward, spontaneous obedience to God in the power of Christ's Holy Spirit, the mature freedom of the sons and daughters of God.

As the primal sacrament, then, Baptism is, in a special sense, both the sacrament of faith in Christ and the embodiment of that faith. That is why, should circumstances make Baptism impossible, faith alone can impart fellowship with Christ and redemption through what is called "Baptism of desire." One who truly believes in the Lord is prepared to do his bidding without reserve and, therefore, wishes, so far is possible, to receive Baptism.

He or she is not saved without the desire (at least implicit) of Baptism. At once justified in this way, he or she must still receive the sacrament, for it incorporates him or her into the Church's visible communion, thus entitling him or her to take part in all its sacramental and liturgical life in Christ.

--Burkhard Neunheuser, Encyclopedia of Theology, pages 66-75, edited by Patrick J. Hession

The Eucharist: Sacrament of Unity or Symbol of Division?

On the night before he died, Jesus met with his apostles for the last time and celebrated a meal with them. During that meal, he took bread, blessed it, broke it, and said, "Take it: this is my Body." Then, he took a cup of wine, gave thanks, and gave it to them, and they all drank from it. He said to them, "This is my Blood of the Covenant, which will be shed on behalf of many for the forgiveness of sins. Do this in remembrance of me" (Mark 14:22-24; Matthew 26:26-28; Luke 22:14-20; 1 Corinthians 11:23-26).

In this action, Jesus established a means of our achieving intimate and personal union with him in his own death and Resurrection. He gave himself to us as food and drink, his own Body and Blood, his very own Person. Or did he? Did he mean what he said, that this bread and wine are truly his

Body and Blood, his own Person, or was he speaking only symbolically?

While almost all Christians celebrate this ritual, variously called the Last Supper, the Breaking of Bread, Holy Communion, Mass, or the Lord's Table, much controversy has arisen over the last centuries, especially since the Reformation, about what it all means. Are we to use bread and wine, as Jesus did, or will a cracker and grape juice suffice? Should the bread be leavened? Should it be a loaf or flat, like pita? Or should it be unleavened? Does it really matter? Does the bread remain bread or does it become his real Body? Does the wine remain wine or does it become his real Blood?

These are questions that have divided Christians for much too long! If Jesus intended the Eucharist to be a source of union with him and with one another, why has it become a symbol of division among those who profess to be his followers? Is this not a scandal to the unbeliever, or even to the simple believer who desires an intimate relationship with the risen Lord? If the bread and wine truly *is* the real Body and Blood, the Person of Jesus, are not those who profess to be their spiritual leaders short-changing their followers out of something that is essential to their spiritual growth and relationship with their Lord? If so, *by what right and authority do they do this*? It is time to take another, deeper look at what Jesus had in mind when he gave us this command: "Do this in remembrance of me." What did he mean by *this*?

The Eucharist in the History of the Church

Having concluded the prayers, we greet one another with a kiss. Then, there is brought to the president of the brethren bread and a cup of water and of watered wine. Taking them, he gives praise and glory to the Father of all, through the Name of the Son and of the Holy Spirit. He himself gives thanks at some length in order that these things may be deemed worthy. When the prayers and the thanksgiving are completed, all people present call out their assent, saying, "Amen!" "Amen" in the Hebrew language signifies "so be it." After the president has given thanks, and all the people have shouted their assent, those whom we call deacons give to each one present to partake of the Eucharistic Bread and Wine and water. To those who are absent they carry away a portion.

We call this food Eucharist, and no one else is permitted to partake of it except one who believes our teaching to be true and who has been washed in the washing that is for the remission of sins and for regeneration, and is, thereby, living as Christ has enjoined. Not as common bread nor common drink do we receive these, but since Jesus Christ our Savior was made incarnate by the word of God and had both flesh and blood for our salvation, so too, as we have been taught, the food that has been made into the Eucharist by the Eucharistic prayer set down by him, and by the change of which our blood and flesh is nourished, is both the Flesh and Blood of that incarnate Jesus.

The apostles, in the Memoirs that they produced which are called Gospels, have, thus, passed on that which was enjoined on them: that Jesus took bread and, having given thanks, said, "Do this in remembrance of me; this is my Body." And in like manner, taking the cup, and having given thanks, he said, "This is my Blood."

St. Justin the Martyr, c100-165, *First Apology* 66

I have no taste for corruptible food or for the pleasures of this life. I desire the Bread of God, which is the Flesh of Jesus Christ, who was the seed of David, and for drink I desire his Blood, which is love incorruptible. Take care, then, to use one Eucharist so that, whatever you do, you do according to God.

There is one Flesh of our Lord Jesus Christ and one cup in the union of his Blood. There is one altar as there is one bishop, with the presbytery and my fellow servants, the deacons. The Eucharist is the Flesh of our Savior Jesus Christ, Flesh which suffered for our sins and which the Father, in his goodness, raised up.

St. Ignatius, third bishop of Antioch, *Letter to the Philadelphians* 3

They (the Donatists) abstain from the Eucharist

and prayers because they do not admit that the Eucharist is the Flesh of our savior Jesus Christ, who suffered for our sins, whom the Father in his goodness raised up.

St. Ignatius, *Letter to the Smyrnaeans* 6

How will they allow that the bread over which thanksgiving has been said is the Body of their Lord, and that the chalice is the chalice of his Blood if they say that he is not the Son of the creator of the world, that is to say, his Word through whom the tree bears fruit, and the fountains flow, and the earth yields first the blade, then the ear, then the full corn in the ear?

Just as the bread of the earth, receiving the invocation of God, is no longer common bread but Eucharist, consisting of two things, an earthly and a heavenly, so also our bodies, partaking of the Eucharist, are no longer corruptible, having the hope of eternal resurrection.

If the body is not saved, then, in fact, neither did the Lord redeem us with his Blood; neither is the cup of the Eucharist the partaking of his Blood nor is the Bread which we break the partaking of his Body. He has declared the cup, a part of creation, to be his own Blood from which he causes our blood to flow and the bread, a part of creation, he has established as his own Body from which he gives increase to our bodies.

St. Irenaeus, second bishop of Lyons, 140-202, *Against Heretics* 18, 5 & 6

If Christ Jesus our Lord and God is himself the high priest of God the Father and first offered himself as a sacrifice to the Father and commanded that this be done in remembrance of himself, then, assuredly, the priest acts truly in Christ's place when he imitates what Christ did, and he offers, then, a true and complete sacrifice to God the Father if he offers as he sees Christ himself has offered.

Cyprian, Bishop of Carthage, 248-258, *Epistle on the Eucharist* 43, 14

Let us, then, with full confidence, partake of the Body and Blood of Christ. In the figure of bread his Body is given to you, and in the figure of wine his Blood is given to you so that, by partaking of the Body and Blood of Christ, you might become united in body and blood with him.

Thus, do we become Christ-bearers, his Body and Blood being distributed through our members. And, thus, it is that we become, according to the blessed Peter, sharers of the divine nature. Do not, therefore, regard the bread and the wine as simply that: they are, according to the Master's declaration, the Body and Blood of Christ.

Even though the senses suggest to you the other,

let faith make you firm. Do not judge in this matter by taste but be fully assured by the faith, not doubting that you have been deemed worthy of the Body and Blood of Christ

St. Cyril, a bishop of Jerusalem, 315-386 A.D. *Catechesis* 22

We believe that the Word became flesh and that we receive his Flesh in the Lord's Supper. How, then, can we fail to believe that he really dwells within us? When he became man, he actually clothed himself in our flesh, uniting it to himself forever. In the sacrament of his Body, he actually gives us his own Flesh, which he has united to his divinity. This is why we are all one, because the Father is in Christ, and Christ is in us.

St. Hilary of Poitiers, c 315-c 368. *On the Holy Trinity,* Book 8

The Lord Jesus himself declares, "This is my Body." Before the blessing of the heavenly words, another species is mentioned; after the consecration, the Body is signified. He himself speaks of his Blood. Before the consecration, it is mentioned as something else; after the consecration, it is called Blood. And you say, "Amen," that is, "It is true." What the mouth speaks, let the mind within confess; what words utter, let the heart feel.

St. Ambrose, c 340-397, *The Mysteries,* Chapter 9

Creator and Lord of all things, whatever their nature, he brought forth bread from the earth and changed it into his own Body. Not only had he the power to do this, but also he had promised it. As he had changed water into wine, he also changed wine into his own Blood.

St. Gaudentius of Brescia, d 413, *Treatise 2*

Terminology: The Beginning of Controversy

The doctrine of the Eucharist was not a subject of controversy in the first centuries. Therefore, the need for a precise formulation did not arise. The tendency to advance from the *assertion* of the real presence of Christ's flesh and blood to a precise theory of the *mode* of this presence in the elements was more marked in the East than in the West.

Peter Lombard, the most influential theologian of the twelfth century, maintained the "substantial" presence of Christ's Body under the accidents of the elements.

The term "transubstantiation" seems to have been adopted in the twelfth century. But, it is impossible to say when it came to have a technical meaning, that is, to convey more than the assertion that the elements after consecration are "really" the Body and the Blood.

In 1215, the Fourth Lateran Council decreed that "the Body and the Blood are truly contained in the sacrament of the altar under the species of bread and wine; the bread being transubstantiated into the Body and the wine into the Blood by the power of God."

In its technical sense, transubstantiation denotes a doctrine that is based on the Aristotelian philosophy as taught by the schoolmen, or Scholastics as they were called. According to this philosophy, a physical object consists of "accidents," the properties that are observed or perceived by the senses, and an underlying "substance," in which the accidents inhere and which gives to the object its essential nature. According to the doctrine of transubstantiation, the accidents of bread and wine remain after consecration, but their substance is changed into that of the Body and Blood of Christ.

In 1539, King Henry VIII, later the first head of the Church of England, affirmed this same doctrine in the Six Articles: "The most blessed sacrament of the altar, by the strength and efficacy of Christ's mighty word (it being spoken by the priest), is present really, under the form of bread and wine, the natural Body and Blood of our savior Jesus Christ, conceived of the virgin Mary. After the consecration, there remains no substance of bread or wine or any other substance but the substance of Christ, God and man. It is to be believed and not doubted that, in the Flesh, under the form of bread, is the very Blood, and with the Blood, under the form of wine, is the very

Flesh, each separately as though they were both together."

On this point, then, and at this time, Christians of both East and West were in agreement. In October, 1551, the Council of Trent reaffirmed the Lateran Council decree: "Since Christ our Redeemer said that that which he offered under the appearance of bread and wine was truly his Body, it has, therefore, always been held in the Church of God, and this holy Synod now declares anew, that, through the consecration of the bread and wine, there comes about a conversion of the whole substance of the bread into the substance of the Body of Christ the Lord, and of the whole substance of the wine into the substance of his Blood. The Holy Catholic Church conveniently and properly called this conversion "transubstantiation." In the venerable sacrament of the Eucharist, then, the whole Christ is contained under each species and in each separate part of each species" (Session XIII).

--compiled and edited by Patrick J. Hession

The Institution of the Eucharist by the Historical Jesus

The Church celebrates the Eucharist by virtue of the authority and the commission expressly given to it by Jesus. The institution of the supper by the historical Jesus is decisive for all Eucharistic practice and dogma. The institution of the

Church's supper by the historical Jesus appears today to be of particular importance. The following provides an in-depth exploration of the meaning underlying this important doctrine and practice.

Our earliest witness, Paul, expressly traces his account of the institution back to a received tradition, one that ultimately derived from Jesus: "For I received from the Lord what I also handed on to you, that the Lord Jesus, on the night he was betrayed, took bread, and, after he had given thanks, broke it and said, 'This is my Body that is for you. Do this in remembrance of me.' In the same way, also, the cup, after supper, saying, 'This cup is the New Covenant in my Blood. Do this, as often as you drink it, in remembrance of me.' For as often as you eat this bread and drink the cup, you proclaim the death of the Lord until he comes" (1 Corinthians 11:23-26).

This claim is strengthened by characteristics that are typical of Jesus' manner of speech: "I tell you, I shall not eat it [again] until there is fulfillment in the kingdom of God. I tell you that, from now on, I shall not drink of the fruit of the vine until the kingdom of God comes" (Luke 22:16, 18). "Amen, I say to you, I shall not drink again of the fruit of the vine until the day when I drink it new in the kingdom of God" (Mark 14:25). In the Aramaic turns of speech within *all* the accounts, their Semitic origin is recognizable, and their date and form can be traced to the forties.

A further pointer to the historical Jesus is the fact that both of the existing strands of the tradition, that of Paul-Luke, and that of Mark-Matthew, differ according to the *formulation* and the *theology* but agree in their understanding of the *essential meaning* of the supper. The difference of the formulations can be traced to the transmitters of the tradition. The agreement as to the supper's meaning, however, must be traced to Jesus as the source of the tradition.

Finally, it is precisely the presence of the supper in the life of Jesus, and the light thrown on it by Jesus' life as a whole, that disclose the true character of the sacrament and that make consistent explanation possible.

Jesus' Life and Purpose

Jesus accomplished the decisive purpose of his life, his task as Messiah, in carrying out the mission of the Servant of God of Deutero-Isaiah, who, as God's majestic envoy, proclaims and inaugurates a new phase of salvation, and who, as martyr, takes upon himself expiatory sufferings for the sins of many.

As his life went on, Jesus thought frequently of his death and spoke often of it to his disciples. It was, for Jesus, not something that merely happened to him. It was a conscious and willed deed to which he assented as a necessity in the history of salvation and on which he freely decided: "There is a baptism with which I must be baptized, and how great is my anguish until it is accomplished!" (Luke 12:50).

His total readiness for the death, which was the mission of the Servant of the Lord, is also expressed in the teaching of the ransom ("The Son of Man did not come to be served but to serve and to give his life as a ransom for many" Mark 10:45), and the prophecies of the passion ("He began to teach them that the Son of Man must suffer greatly and be rejected by the elders, the chief priests, and the scribes, and be killed, and rise after three days." "He was teaching his disciples and telling them, 'The Son of Man is to be handed over to men, and they will kill him, and three days after his death he will rise.' " "Behold, we are going up to Jerusalem, and the Son of Man will be handed over to the chief priests and the scribes, and they will condemn him to death, and they will mock him, spit upon him, scourge him, and put him to death. After three days, he will rise" Mark 8:31, 9:31, 10:33 & 34).

These are, at their core, genuine prophecies of Jesus but, in their New Testament form, represent interpretative elaborations of the early Church based on its knowledge of the actual course of the passion.

Jesus maintained his obedient "yes" to vicarious

expiation through all outward and inward afflictions, even in the dread of death, torments, and abandonment by God. His death is the total dedication and the deepest fulfillment of his being.

Besides his death, Jesus also foretold his Resurrection. In Jesus' prophecies of resurrection, we hear the victorious certainty that his death, which he took upon himself purely out of desire for atonement and in eager obedience to the will of the Father, would find recognition before God. Here, the one who offers himself functions, also, as the gift in his own Person and accomplished the sacrificial dedication by the real shedding of his blood.

Jesus must have been sure that God would accept his sacrifice, his body, and, hence, that God would fill it with new life. Thus, the death of Jesus brings with it the Resurrection as an inner consequence, as an essential part of it, regardless of the difference in time between the two events.

For the fourth evangelist, the lifting up of Jesus on the Cross already means his being lifted up in glory ("Just as Moses lifted up the serpent in the desert, so must the Son of Man be lifted up so that everyone who believes in him may have eternal life." "So Jesus said, 'When you lift up the Son of Man, then you will realize that I AM, and that I do nothing on my own, but I say only what the Father taught me." "'And when I am lifted up from the earth, I will draw everyone to myself.' He said this, indicating the kind of death he would die" John 3:14, 8:28, 12:32 & 33).

In this readiness for death, and in the certain conviction that the sacrifice of his life would be accepted by God and lead to a new order of salvation, Jesus celebrated his last supper and established it as his Testament. He summed up in it a visible and even edible blessing and bequeathed them as a sacrament.

Hence, the supper must not only be explained in the light of the entire life of Jesus, it *is* this entirety in symbolic compression. Its meaning is already partly indicated by its character as a farewell meal. ("He said to them, 'I have eagerly desired to eat this Passover with you before I suffer'" Luke 22:15).

The last celebration of Jesus, according to the synoptics, is the paschal, or Passover, meal, while, according to John 18:28, it takes place before the official paschal date. At any rate, its date is near to that of the Pasch, is influenced by it (the explanation of the foods and the sequence of bread-meal-cup), and is permeated by the spiritual atmosphere of the Jewish feast as a cultic memorial of the saving deed of Yahweh. The New Testament, however, nowhere interprets the Eucharist in the light of the Passover. Rather, a key for the understanding of the supper is given in the biblical idea of the prophetic sign or prophetic action.

The Eucharist as Prophetic Action

This phenomenon is meant not merely as a truth in symbolic dress or the pictorial orientation toward some coming event. It is already the initial realization of a divine decree. An event ordained by God is not merely registered and told of in words; it is brought about and initially realized. The action does not merely represent it symbolically; it anticipates and crystallizes its reality. The prophetic sign is the efficacious sign of a divine action.

Jesus situates his supper within the framework of this specific sphere of a divine causality: a) he announces in words the saving sacrifice of his death, b) he represents it symbolically and makes it present by distributing the food and drink as his Body and Blood, whereby c) he makes of these elements his Person, bodily offered up.

All of the accounts situate the action in the perspective of his death by indicating the time (night of the offering) and by the adjectival phrase at the end of the words over the bread, which is indispensable for the understanding of the action: "given for many." In a clear allusion to Isaiah 53:12 ("Therefore, I will give him his portion among the great, and he shall divide the spoils with the mighty because he surrendered himself to death and was counted among the wicked; and he shall take away the sins of many and win pardon for their offenses"), Jesus' death appears here as the martyr's sacrifice of his Person, who is the Suffering Servant of God.

The same notion is conjured up by the second expression: "This cup of the new covenant in my Blood." The predicate "the new covenant" takes up the title from Isaiah 42:6 ("I, the Lord, have called you for the victory of justice. I grasped you by the hand. I formed you and set you as a covenant of the people, a light for the nations"), characterizing Jesus as the founder of a covenant. He fulfills this task, however, "in his blood," i.e. by shedding his blood.

The biblical term "blood" has the connotation of "shed," as the addition "shed for many" in Mark 14:24 indicates, that is, instead of and for the sake of the whole of mankind. This, too, is dependent on Isaiah 53:10 & 11 ("If he gives his life as an offering for sin, he shall see his descendants in a long life, and the will of the Lord shall be accomplished through him. Because of his affliction, he shall see the light in fullness of days. Through his suffering, my servant will justify many, and their guilt he shall bear"). Thus, in all of the accounts, the death of Jesus is the determinant factor in the Last Supper.

The sacrificial death thus announced in words by Jesus was also the object of a symbolic action. He actualized the offering of his Person to the Father for people by consecrating bread and wine as his own Person and by giving them to be eaten by people. His taking and lifting up of the elements, their blessing and consecration as his Body and Blood, means their transfer to God and displays Jesus' dedication to the Father.

When Jesus, then, gives the food and drink as his Body and Blood and gives it to be eaten and drunk by people, he portrays visibly the martyr's death, which is the dedication of his inmost life for people but also its recovery in the Resurrection. Moreover, not only the proffering itself but also the proffering as food and drink reveal how his death, indeed his whole human existence, is for people, in their stead and for their sake.

Just as it is the nature of food and drink to be wholly and entirely for people, and just as they give up their own being to belong to people and to become part of people, thereby building up their life, so, too, Jesus is there for people (by the very fact of his incarnation) and belongs to people. So, too, he gives up his life in order that they may live to God.

Finally, however, the proffered elements of the meal are not merely an outward means of representing his sacrificial offering on the cross. They are identical with the one and the same sacrificial gift of the Cross, this man Jesus. Hence, the inner identity of both actions and the actual presence of the bloody offering of himself on the Cross is established and finally assured in the un-bloody offering of himself in the meal.

By the divine power of his determinative words, Jesus changes the bread and wine into his own sacrificed Person. The term "body" means, in the mouth of Jesus as a rendering of the Semitic expression behind it, not only a part of a person, as though his body were distinguished from his blood or soul, but the whole person in his bodily existence.

Likewise, the "blood," for the Semites, represents the life-substance ("But make sure that you do not partake of the blood, therefore, for blood is life, and you shall consume this seat of life with the flesh" Deuteronomy 12:23. "Since the life of a living body is in its blood, I have made you put it on the altar so that atonement may, thereby, be made for your own lives because it is the blood as the seat of life that makes atonement." "Since the life of every living body is its blood, anyone who partakes of it shall be cut off" Leviticus 17:11, 14a) and stands for the living being with blood coursing through its veins, especially when it suffers a violent death ("The Lord then said [to Cain], 'What have you done! Listen: your brother's blood cries out to me from the soil!" Genesis 4:10. [Judas] said: "I have sinned in betraying innocent blood" Matthew 27:4. "And, the whole people said in reply, 'His blood be upon us and upon our children!' " Matthew 27:25. "Yet, you have filled Jerusalem with your teaching and want to bring this man's blood upon you" Acts 5:28). It indicates, then, the person in the act of shedding his blood.

The adjectival addition to the words over the bread and the cup ("which will be given for you" Luke 22:19, "which will be shed for many" Mark 14:24), as also the early apostolic description of the cup as "the new covenant," defines the Person of Jesus more precisely as the savior who is the Servant of God.

The essential identity of the consecrated elements with the Person of Jesus is indicated in the sentence structure of the blessing, which differs from purely metaphorical statements. In the words of consecration, we have, in contrast to metaphors, a subject ("this") that is, of itself, colorless and indeterminate but that is defined by a very concrete predicate ("my Body," "my Blood").

The real presence of Jesus can be better explained from the character of the supper as a prophetic sign in which both action and word bring about, through divine power, what they represent. It is supported by the act of distribution that underlines the nature ascribed to the gifts and also by the fact that they are partaken of. Exegetically, this is ultimately assured by the normative interpretation of the supper in the New Testament in terms of the real presence, especially in Paul and John.

Hence, the bodily Person of Jesus is present in the supper not, however, in the static manner of being of a thing but as the Servant of God who, in his sacrificial death, brings about the salvation of us all and, more precisely, as the sacrificial offering of the Servant who delivers himself up on the Cross. The real presence of the person is there to actualize the presence of the sacrificial deed and is united with this in an organic whole. The Eucharist becomes, then, the abiding presence in the meal of the sacrificially constituted saving event "Jesus," in whom Person and work form an inseparable unity.

The inaugurative command, "do this in remembrance of me," gives the Church the power to do what Jesus did. By this command, the re-enactments must be formally similar to the initial supper celebrated by Jesus. It gives these re-enactments the divinely-effective power of Jesus' supper and emphasizes and assures their identity of substance with the first supper and with each other. It characterizes them as the *anamnesis* of Jesus.

Anamnesis, in the biblical sense, means not only the subjective representation of something in the consciousness and as an act of the remembering mind. It is also the objective effectiveness and presence of one reality in another, especially in the effectiveness and presence of the saving actions of God in the liturgical worship. Even in the Old Testament, the liturgy is the privileged medium in which the covenant attains actuality.

The Eucharist in Paul and John

Besides the narratives of the institution, the New

Testament itself explains Jesus' acts in a way that is fundamental and normative for all exegesis and dogmatic theology. Paul affirms the bodily real presence of Jesus when he teaches that the bread which is broken and the cup which is blessed is a sharing in the Body and Blood of Jesus ("The cup of blessing that we bless, is it not a partaking in the Blood of Christ? The bread that we break, is it not a participation in the Body of Christ?" 1 Corinthians 10:16), when he concludes to the unity of all Christians as one single Body (of Christ) from their partaking of the one Bread ("Because the loaf of bread is one, we, though many, are one Body for we all partake of the one loaf" 10:17), and when he points to the unworthy reception of the Body of Jesus as explanation of certain judgments of God. ("Therefore, whoever eats the bread or drinks the cup of the Lord unworthily will have to answer for the Body and Blood of the Lord. A person should examine himself or herself and so eat the bread and drink the cup. For anyone who eats and drinks without discerning the Body eats and drinks judgment on himself or herself. That is why many of you are ill and infirm, and a considerable number are dying. If we discerned ourselves, we would not be under judgment. But, since we are judged by [the] Lord, we are being disciplined along with the world" 1 Corinthians 11:27-31). Insofar as he places the Lord's Supper in relation to Jewish and heathen sacrificial meals (1 Corinthians 10:18-22), he presents it as a sacrificial action. A sacrificial meal presupposes and brings with it the killing of the victim.

John does not give an account of the institution but gives a detailed proclamation of the Eucharist in the great promissory discourse of 6:26-63, which is conceived throughout in the perspective of a sacrament. Its theme is the true bread of heaven. The spiritual reality of this bread, its heavenly origin and its power to mediate life, is there in the historical man Jesus (John 6:26-51b), but the physical reality, as food in the literal sense, is there in his "Flesh," which is intended for the life of the world and which one must really eat ("chew"), just as one must also drink his Blood as real drink ("I am the living bread that came down from heaven. Whoever eats this bread will live forever, and the bread that I will give is my Flesh for the life of the world. The Jews quarreled among themselves, saying, 'How can this man give us [his] Flesh to eat?' Jesus said to them, 'Amen, amen, I say to you, unless you eat the Flesh of the Son of Man and drink his Blood, you do not have life within you. Whoever eats my Flesh and drinks my Blood has eternal life, and I will raise him or her up on the last day for my Flesh is true food, and my Blood is true drink. Whoever eats my Flesh and drinks my Blood remains in me, and I in him or her. Just as the living Father sent me, and I have life because of the Father, so also the one who feeds on me will have life because of me. This is the bread that came down from heaven. Unlike your ancestors who ate and still died, whoever eats this Bread will live forever' " John 6:51-58).

Such partaking, however, presupposes the

sacrifice. The surprising term "flesh," even in connection with "blood," is not a sacrificial element distinct from the blood but the whole concrete man Jesus, as John 1:14 ("and the Word became flesh and made his dwelling among us") and the personal pronoun ("whoever eats me") in 6:57 show.

In the Eucharist, the descent of Jesus from the heavenly world, his incarnation for the purpose of the sacrificial offering, remains present (6:57ff). But, the ascension of Jesus is also effective there, ("What if you were to see the Son of Man ascending to where he was before?" 6:62) since the ascension alone makes the sending of the Spirit possible ("Let anyone who thirsts come to me and drink. Whoever believes in me, as Scripture says, 'Rivers of living water will flow from within him.' He said this in reference to the Spirit that those who came to believe in him were to receive" John 7:38 & 39; see also John 16:7) and hence, also, our sacramental meal ("It is the spirit that gives life, while the flesh is of no avail. The words I have spoken to you are spirit and life." John 6:63).

The element that really mediates life there is not the flesh as such but the accompanying Spirit, by which the Godhead in Jesus is meant ("The first man, Adam, became a living being; the last Adam a life-giving spirit. But, the spiritual was not first. Rather, the natural and then the spiritual. The first man was from the earth, earthly; the second man from heaven" 1 Corinthians 15:45-47). For John, too, the Eucharist remains the presence, in the liturgical meal, of the economy of salvation which is "Jesus."

Conclusion

To conclude, then, the essentials of the Lord's Supper were unalterably prescribed for the Church by Jesus, the consecration of the bread and wine (unleavened bread, if it was the Passover meal) to be his Body and Blood and their distribution to be eaten and drunk. This decisive core, however, was given a liturgical framework that underwent a development in both the East and the West.

After the words of consecration, the same words that Jesus used, whatever makes bread to be bread is no longer there but is now the Body and Blood of the Person Jesus; and whatever makes wine to be wine is no longer there but is now the Body and Blood of the Person Jesus.

It is the real Body and Blood of the Person Jesus that is eaten and drunk, separately or together, so that the person who eats and/or drinks is *truly* united with the Person of Jesus, not just *symbolically*. This is what Jesus intended when he instituted this sacrament and what the believer must understand and accept. Anything less diminishes the meaning and intent of the one who gave himself in this sacrament for our salvation.

--Johannes Betz, Encyclopedia of Theology, pages 448-453, edited by Patrick J. Hession

The Mother of Jesus in Scripture and in the Church

Mary, the mother of Jesus (Mark 6:8; Matthew 13:55; Acts 1:4), does not figure largely in the New Testament writings. The testimonies of faith in her regard take on greater extent and depth with the growing interest in the life of Jesus, his death and Resurrection being the event first and primarily proclaimed in Scripture.

Yet, there is no reason to ignore her existence and importance simply because of often-erroneous perceptions of Catholic excesses. An objective study reveals that she has much to teach any Christian who desires to be a sincere follower and disciple of her Son.

In the letters of Paul, which are earlier than the gospels, Mary is mentioned only in Galatians 4:4, but the important truth is already uttered here.

Paul speaks of the Messiah by speaking of Mary, though without mentioning her name: "When the fullness of time had come, God sent his Son, born of a woman, born under the law." According to this text, Mary is the place in which the Son of God entered human history. The birth from a woman guarantees the true humanity and historicity of the crucified and risen Lord, whom Paul preaches, and excludes all "spiritualizing" tendencies.

When Christians began to have recourse to the life and actions of Jesus before his death and Resurrection, the mother of Jesus, who was part of his life, began to play a greater role. This new interest was satisfied most fully in the gospels of Matthew and Luke (about A.D. 80), which narrate the conception and birth of Jesus. They do not confine themselves like Mark to scenes from the public life of Jesus.

According to the gospel of Mark (3:20f; 3:31-35), Jesus' relatives, and also his mother, whose participation, however, was merely that of a silent bystander, sought to fetch Jesus back home since his activity was arousing the crowds and drawing attention.

Matthew (12:46-50) and Luke (8:19f) present this text in such a way as to lessen the awkwardness for Christian readers. Luke gives another scene from the public life of Jesus. He relates that, when a woman praised his mother, he responded by saying, "Yes, blessed indeed are they who hear the word of God and observe it" (Luke 11:28).

Interest in the beginning of the life of the Messiah led to the composition of the infancy narratives in Matthew 1 and 2 and Luke 1 and 2. They diverge from each other in many ways, especially the genealogies, so that the stories cannot be fully harmonized. The two evangelists were obviously drawing on different streams of tradition. Further, each evangelist had a theological purpose, which meant that the traditions were placed in a theological perspective. Both infancy narratives have Old Testament and Jewish traits, but the historical core remains.

We learn that Mary came from Nazareth and that she was espoused or engaged to Joseph, of the house of David (Matthew 1:18; Luke 1:26f). Whether Mary herself was of the house of David is not clear from the text. Joseph's ancestry was enough to make Jesus legally son of David. Before Mary had been brought to Joseph's house as his married wife, the angel Gabriel announced to her (Luke 1:26ff) that she was most highly favored and that the Lord was with her. She was to conceive and bring forth a son, whom she was to call Jesus. Her motherhood was not to come about through human intervention but through the action of the Holy Spirit (Matthew 1:18; Luke 1:35). The heavenly message telling her that she was to be the mother of the Messiah prompted her to pay a visit to her cousin Elizabeth. The evangelist attributes to Elizabeth, to Mary herself, and to Simeon, as he greets the Messiah in the temple, hymns of praise and thanks that are mosaics of the Old Testament elements.

The birth takes place in Bethlehem (Matthew 1:23; 2:1; Luke 1:27; 2:4). Shepherds come to pay homage to the child, and wise men come from the East. Herod's murderous intentions force Mary to take refuge in Egypt. When the family returns, Mary lives at Nazareth with Jesus and Joseph (Matthew 2:23; Luke 2:38). Jesus was circumcised and presented in the temple according to the prescriptions of the law (Luke 2:21-40).

Only one other scene from the childhood of Jesus is narrated, the visit to the temple in Jerusalem (Luke 2:41-52). It is a striking scene because, instead of joining the returning pilgrims and without warning his parents, Jesus stayed behind. When his parents found him after an anxious search, he gave them the astonishing answer, "Why were you looking for me? Did you not know that I must be in my Father's house?" As the evangelist says, Mary and Joseph did not understand, but Mary kept all these things in her heart, to meditate on them in faith.

One particular question forces itself upon our attention in the story of the infancy. It is that of the virginal conception and birth. Why should

Mary have let herself be espoused if she had no intention of leading a married life? Hence, many theologians now assume that Mary resolved on a life of virginity only at the moment of the annunciation. She then dedicated herself exclusively and without reserve to the service of the divine plan of salvation. Through this dedication, she conceived the Son of God in her spirit as well as in her body.

The Holy Spirit is here represented not as the father who begets Jesus but as an active force which brings about the conception. The notion of procreation without a father is foreign to the Old Testament. It also differs essentially from pagan mythology, according to which a god unites himself to an earthly woman and begets a child like an earthly father. Hence, the virginal conception and birth of Jesus must be considered as a revelation proper to the New Testament.

Nonetheless, this revelation was prepared for in the Old Testament narratives in which great men were born of mothers who were, humanly speaking, doomed to sterility (Genesis 18; 1 Samuel 1). The promise of the Messiah in Isaiah 7:14, which speaks of the bringer of salvation and his birth from a woman, was probably already understood by the Greek translators of the Septuagint as a prophecy of the virginal birth. This, at any rate, is the meaning given to the text of Isaiah in Matthew.

If one asks why Jesus should have been virginally conceived, the answer is not that an earthly father would have been a sort of unwelcome rival to the heavenly Father of the preexistent Word. Nor is it that conception in the course of marriage would have been unworthy of the eternal Son of God. The reason is the transparency with which the virginal conception and birth lets the creative power of God and his sole initiative in the work of salvation shine through. No human deed occasions it.

It is part of the most ancient faith of the Church that, after the birth of Jesus, her first-begotten (Luke 1:7; cf. Matthew 1:25), Mary renounced married intercourse with Joseph in consequence of her total dedication to the charge given her by God and, hence, to God himself.

The "brothers of Jesus" who are mentioned several times in Scripture (Mark 3:31; 6:3; John 2:12; Acts 1:14; 1 Corinthians 9:5; Galatians 1:19) could be the actual brothers of Jesus as far as the literal sense of the texts is concerned but, according to biblical Greek, they need only have been cousins of Jesus (Genesis 13:8; 14:14). Catholic exegetes take the latter meaning. Then, according to Mark 6:3; 15:40, Mary, the mother of the brothers of Jesus, is different from the mother of Jesus himself.

The Acts and the Gospel of John provide further information. According to Acts, Mary was with the disciples of Jesus at Jerusalem as they awaited the coming of the Holy Spirit promised by Jesus (Acts 1:14). According to John, Mary took part in the marriage feast of Cana (John 2:1-11). She asks Jesus to come to the aid of the hosts, whose wine has run out. Jesus first refused his mother's request and then grants it. Mary appears here as the lady of the house. It is obvious that, at the time when the fourth gospel was composed, Mary's place was fully recognized in the Church (Bultmann).

Under the cross (cf. John 19:25ff), her dying Son tells Mary that she is now to consider the beloved disciple as her son. Jesus tells the disciple that he must consider Mary as his mother. The transparently symbolic character of the fourth gospel allows us to conclude that the words of Jesus go beyond the purely historical and point to the relationship between Mary and the Church.

The doctrine of the Church emerges as follows: Mary conceived Jesus the Messiah through the Holy Spirit and is, therefore, truly bringer-forth and mother of God. In and after the birth of Jesus, she remained a virgin. It may be affirmed that Mary's giving birth was a fully human and personal act and that, even as a bodily process, it was entirely determined by the grace of her motherhood, though it is impossible to indicate precisely the nature of the virginity of the birth. It may be said that Mary conceived Jesus of the Holy Spirit without a male principle of generation.

It is the constant teaching of the Church from the beginning that she gave birth to Jesus without violation of her integrity and that she remained ever virgin. Though there has been no formal definition on the subject, the perpetual virginity of Mary is part of the faith and preaching of the Church.

Mary entered into the process of salvation through her faith. As the Fathers frequently affirmed, she first conceived the Son of God and savior in her heart through faith and then in her body. By her "Let it be done" to the divine message, Mary contributed to salvation, just as Eve had to man's ruin. This does not mean that God made his plan of salvation dependent on Mary's consent but that, according to the eternal plan of salvation, man, for his part, was to assent to salvation through divine grace.

Humanity's *yes* to God and to Christ the savior is summed up in Mary. In her acceptance of God's plan for her by faith, she received salvation for all. Mary's participation is founded on the fact that she gave life to the historical bringer of salvation and followed his work in faith and love to the death of the cross. But this was not all. The salvation brought by Christ is ordained to each person by its very constitution. It calls for acceptance and assimilation. This is where its essential purpose is fulfilled.

Mary was the primary recipient of his salvation,

which she took to herself in the most excellent way, not only for herself in individualistic isolation but also with a willingness and an openness that were oriented to all people.

Her personal appropriation of salvation has significance for the whole Church. Salvation is present and accessible in the Church, the Body of Christ, and Mary is the first and most privileged member of the Church. The Church is the Body of which Christ is the Head, and the Church is the Bride of whom Christ is the Bridegroom.

The first image is not meant to point to a natural but to a personal relationship, and the second is even more explicitly personal. They both mean that the Church, the fellowship of the faithful, is called to bring about and maintain the saving bond with the savior and that this is its responsibility.

Mary was the type or model of all in pronouncing her "Let it be done" both of those who already belong to the Church and of all others insofar as all are called to the Church, that is, to Christ. But, it would be wrong to see Mary's role in such a way that the immediate relationship to Christ and, in him, to God would be obscured. The function of Mary means that dedication to Christ has a Marian coloring but not that it loses any of its directness.

Mary is where the salvation of Christ came to people in the world, not just as an objective entity but also as the movement of Christ toward people.

That this is involved in the relationship of Mary to Christ is particularly clear from the fact that she was with the disciples in Jerusalem, awaiting the descent of the Holy Spirit (Acts 1:14). She was not invited to the Last Supper, but her presence is noted with some emphasis as the Holy Spirit was awaited.

She knew the power of the Spirit from her own experience since the annunciation. In the Spirit, Jesus himself remained present in the fellowship of the Church. That Mary was there when the Church was constituted in the Holy Spirit, in the Spirit of Christ, is significant for the whole course of its history.

Now, in his presence in heaven, her loving gaze is fixed forever on her risen Son and on his brothers and sisters. But, her whole glorified existence is also praise, thanksgiving, and intercession before God. What she is, she is through Christ. What she does, she does through Christ.

People do not receive salvation as individuals or monads in isolation from one another but as social beings. Each one who receives this gift of salvation becomes also a source of salvation. The good of one is fertile in good things for the other. This general principle holds true for Mary in a special and comprehensive way. Mary's heavenly life of dedication to Christ is marked by her care for the brothers and sisters of her Son who are still on their pilgrim way to the Father. Her existence is perfect exchange of love and also hopeful concern.

The function of Mary in salvation determines her relation to the Church. At a very early date, Mary was regarded as a type or model of the Church, and the Church as the image of Mary. Mary is type or model in her motherly fruitfulness and virginal integrity. In the tradition of the Church, especially in Augustine, Mary's motherhood of Jesus expands to the spiritual motherhood of all the faithful. Her virginity is displayed in her total dedication to God. The Church, in turn, mediates the salvation of Christ through its preaching and the sacrament of Baptism.

It, thus, brings forth the Son of God by grace in people. The Church is virginal because it remains true in faith, in the loving acceptance of God mediated by Christ. Hence, the Church has a Marian life inasmuch as it contemplates, grasps, and proclaims the salvation of Christ realized in Mary.

--Michael Schmaus, Encyclopedia of Theology, pages 893-901, edited by Patrick J. Hession

The Ministering Body of Christ: A Call to Action

Exorbitant medical and housing costs - Downsizing and job insecurity - Social Security uncertainty - Limited welfare, unemployment, and Medicare benefits - Worldwide political, economic, and social instability - Terrorism - Drugs out of control - Floods - Blizzards - Storms - Volcanoes - Hurricanes - Forest fires - Droughts - Crop damage - Widespread famines - Bankruptcies – What in the World Is Going On?

In 1982, while I was living in Raleigh, North Carolina, I received the impression one day of Jesus standing off to my right, hands outstretched before him. The thought came, "The Ministering Body of Christ." Jesus Christ, the Lord of heaven and earth, has been warning us of the above events for years in order to prepare us to be the

Ministering Body of Christ in our time.

The Lord says, "I raise my voice, but who listens to me? I cry out, but who hears my word? This is a time of building up and of washing away. This is a time when I establish my kingdom, and every other kingdom collapses. I raise my voice to warn my people, and who takes heed? A cloud hangs over you, a shadow envelopes you. Do you not hear my voice? There is darkness around you.

"Anything that is not built by my hands will be washed away. Anything that does not come from me will not survive. I cry out to you. Do you hear my voice? I raise my voice to save my people, and they don't listen. This is a time of building up and of tearing down. I have to strengthen my people. I have to prevent my people from being torn down. This is an important time for my people. This is a day of decision that cannot be passed by. I raise my voice. I call forth my people. Who will listen to me? Who will respond to my call?

"I shall renew my Church. I shall renew my people. I shall make my people one. I am calling you to turn away from the desires of the world in your lives. I want to transform your lives. My beloved, you my people who stand before me now, hear my word. I shall set my house in order. I shall purify my people. I shall purify my Church. I shall set aside the deceiver, the false prophet, and the false teacher. I shall set aside anything and anyone who stands in the way of my kingdom (1).

"I am going to restore my people and reunite them. I am going to restore to my people the glory that is mine so that the world will not mock or scorn them but may know that I am God and King and that I have come to redeem and to save this earth" (2).

Jesus is the Head of the Church, which is his Body. What Jesus is calling forth is nothing less than for the Church to be the Ministering Body of Christ in our day in a way that it has not been. The world is desperately looking, in these increasingly dark days, for some place or someone to turn to, some alternative that offers life and security.

Before he returned to the Father, Jesus commissioned and empowered the Body of Christ, the Church, to be this alternative. The Body of Christ was to continue his ministry, to take care of the weak ones, to heal the ones that are sick, to bandage the ones that are hurt, to bring back the ones who wander off, and to look for the ones that are lost.

It was Christ's plan that, within his Body, there should be no one who was needy, nor should anyone have to go to the world's systems to get his or her needs met. The Church was to be the Ministering Body of Christ in and to the world, first to her own and then to the unbeliever. The

Church was to be the sign and the prophetic witness to the world of the continuing presence and work of Christ in the world. The Church was gifted with the gifts and ministries of the Holy Spirit to accomplish this work. And now, once again, Jesus is calling his Church to become and to be his ministering Body. This is not the work of our government or of any government.

The Book of Acts shows us a pattern that the early Church established as an alternative to the world of its day. It offers us today the pattern for becoming the ministering Body that Jesus is calling for. Here it is in capsule form:

The Ministering Body of Christ Shares Its Resources

They devoted themselves to the teaching of the apostles, to the communal life, to the breaking of bread, and to the prayers (3). *All who believed were together and had all things in common* (4). *The community of believers was of one heart and mind, and no one claimed that any of his or her possessions was his or her own, but they had everything in common* (5). *There was no needy person among them for those who owned property or houses would sell them, bring the proceeds of the sale and put them at the feet of the apostles, and they were distributed to each according to need* (6). *They would sell their property and possessions and divide them among all according to each one's need* (7).

You may never have to do this, but would you be *willing* to do so if the Lord asked you to? Are you listening to his voice?

Jesus said, *"Give to the one who asks of you and do not turn your back on the one who wants to borrow* (8). *Give to everyone who asks of you, and, from the one who takes what is yours, do not demand it back* (9). St. John said, *"If someone who has worldly means sees a brother in need and refuses him compassion, how can the love of God remain in him or her? Children, let us love not in word or speech but in deed and truth"* (10).

Wouldn't it be marvelous if you responded to someone's need before he or she had to ask for help? Would that people who might be embarrassed to ask for help could receive it without having to ask! Are you that sensitive to the needs of others? To know Christ is to see him in the joys and in the sufferings of another. Are you holding all of your possessions loosely as a good steward, recognizing that it is God who has provided them to you? You may not think you have much yourself, but are you thankful for his provision to you?

The Ministering Body of Christ Prays and Worships Together

Every day, they devoted themselves to meeting together in the temple area and to breaking bread in their homes. They ate their meals with exultation and sincerity of heart, praising God and enjoying favor with all the people (11).

Do your prayer and worship translate into a life that wins the admiration and approval of the people out in your community who see you?

Jesus said, *"You are the salt of the earth. But, if salt loses its taste, with what can it be seasoned? It is no good for anything but to be thrown out and trampled underfoot. You are the light of the world. Your light must shine before others so that they may see your good deeds and glorify your heavenly Father"* (12).

Do you bear the family resemblance of your Father and your Brother, Jesus? Are you letting him transform you into his image by the renewing of your mind?

The Ministering Body of Christ Ministers Effectively

Many signs and wonders were done among the people at the hands of the apostles (13). *Awe and wonder came upon everyone* (14). *Thus, they even carried the sick people out into the streets and laid them on cots and mats. A large number of people from the towns in the vicinity of Jerusalem also gathered, bringing the sick and those disturbed by unclean spirits, and they were* all *cured* (15).

Is the reason we are not seeing this in our cities and towns perhaps due to the lack of unity among the leaders and the people of God? Are we too comfortable with the disunity within the Body of Christ? Are we ourselves even contributing to disunity by our attitude toward our fellow Christians and toward those of other faiths who don't believe as we do? An un-Christlike attitude hinders the work of Jesus in our world.

John 3:16 is often inadequately quoted because it leaves off verse 17, which says, *"God did not send his Son into the world to condemn the world but that the world might be saved through him."* He sends us for the same purpose so that everyone who believes in him will have eternal life and never really die.

The only love of Jesus that most people will experience for the first time is *his love in us* that you and I give to them. But, we cannot give what we do not have.

God Increases His Family

Every day the Lord added to their number those who were being saved (16). *More than ever, believers in the Lord, great numbers of men and women, were added to them* (17). Note: it says "in the Lord," not "in my church" or "in my church doctrine." We need to be very careful that we are bringing new believers into a personal relationship with God, with whom they will spend eternity, not merely into a system of doctrines and traditions.

Doctrines and traditions and rituals are not wrong in themselves. God himself established them for his people after he freed them from the bondage of Egypt in order to give them a way to establish a personal relationship with him. But, those that do not encourage and help develop a personal relationship between the believer and his or her God need to be questioned and, perhaps, discarded lest we be like the Pharisees and the Sadducees.

People, especially young people, are increasingly disillusioned and skeptical. Many of them do not attend church on a regular basis. Is the Ministering Body of Christ not an alternative that they might be looking for? It is, if we will but accept and follow the call of Jesus. It is a radical alternative because it is so contrary to the world's, and even the Church's, present systems. But, is there any better alternative available in our day?

Jesus knows how radical, how counter cultural, it is, and how difficult it will be to respond. He says to us, "I tell you, my people, that there are some who need to understand this: ways you have responded to me in the past, that have seen you through and brought you this far, will no longer see you through. What I call you to is something new, something totally new. Where there is resistance in your hearts and in your groups, lay down that resistance so that I might bring you further along.

"I see each of you where you are. I know where it is hard for you to change and cannot promise you that change will be easy or that it will come immediately. I cannot promise you that it won't be painful for, indeed, it will cost you, but I promise you this: I shall be with you always, and the pain is nothing compared with what I shall give you in return. What you need to lay down, and what you will give up, and what you think it will cost you is nothing compared with the strength you will have when I am finished with you.

"I have looked into your hearts and have seen my image there. Therefore, I declare you a spiritual sacrifice fitting unto me, and I accept you and welcome you more deeply than ever into my heart. I see your will. I see your willingness to serve me and rejoice as I show you to my Father. As you yourself, in your own heart, say 'yes' to every word that I have spoken to you here and to every sign I have shown to you of my plan and of my will, as you say 'yes,' so now do I anoint you with the precious oil of my Spirit and send you forth armed, equipped, and strong to serve me in the days to come. Therefore, cast off every gloom and fear and rejoice for I, the Lord, am leading you against the foe. I am with you. You belong to me. Therefore, rejoice even in the darkness" (18).

(1) Prophecy given at a charismatic conference at

Notre Dame - 1976
(2) Prophecy given at a charismatic conference at Kansas City – 1977
(3) Acts 2:42a
(4) Acts 2:44
(5) Acts 4:32
(6) Acts 4:34-35
(7) Acts 2:45
(8) Matthew 5:42
(9) Luke 6:30
(10) 1 John 3:17-18
(11) Acts 2:46 & 47a
(12) Matthew 5:13 & 14, 16
(13) Acts 5:12a
(14) Acts 2:43
(15) Acts 5:15a, 16
(16) Acts 2:47b
(17) Acts 5:14
(18) Prophecy given at a charismatic conference at Notre Dame - 1976

Church Teaching on the Sanctity of Life

"Human life is sacred because, from its beginning, it involves the creative action of God and remains forever in a special relationship with the Creator, who is its sole end. God alone is the Lord of life from its beginning until its end. No one can, under any circumstance, claim for himself or herself the right directly to destroy an innocent human being" (*The Gift of Life*, introduction, 5).

Of all visible creatures, only human beings are able to know and love their Creator. They are the only creatures on earth that God has willed for their own sake. They alone are called to share, by knowledge and love, in God's own life. It was for this end that they were created, and this is the fundamental reason for their dignity.

The covenant between God and mankind is

interwoven with reminders of God's gift of human life and man's murderous violence: "From man, in regard to his fellow man, I will demand an accounting for human life. If anyone sheds the blood of man, by man shall his blood be shed for, in the image of God, man has been made" (Genesis 9:5 & 6). The Old Testament always considered blood a sacred sign of life (cf. Leviticus 17:14). This teaching remains necessary for all time.

Scripture specifies the prohibition contained in the fifth commandment: "The innocent and the just shall not be put to death" (Exodus 23:7b). Deliberate murder of an innocent person is gravely contrary to the dignity of the human being, to the golden rule, and to the holiness of the Creator. The law forbidding it is universally valid: it obliges each and every one, always and everywhere.

The natural law, present in the heart of each person and established by reason, is universal in its precepts, and its authority extends to all people. It expresses the dignity of the person and determines the basis for his or her fundamental rights and duties. The great Roman Orator, Cicero, put it this way: "For there is at true law: right reason. It is in conformity with nature, is diffused among all people, and is immutable and eternal. Its orders summon to duty. Its prohibitions turn away from offense. To replace it with a contrary law is a sacrilege. Failure to apply even one of its provisions is forbidden. No one can abrogate it entirely" (Cicero, *Republic III, 22, 33*).

In the Sermon on the Mount, the Lord recalls the commandment, "You shall not kill. Whoever kills will be liable to judgment" (Matthew 5:21) and adds to it the proscription of anger, hatred, and vengeance. Going further, Christ asks his disciples to turn the other cheek, to love their enemies (cf. Matthew 5:22-39; 5:44). He did not defend himself and told Peter to leave his sword in its sheath (cf. Matthew 26:52).

Christian prayer extends to the *forgiveness of enemies* (Matthew 5:43 & 44), transfiguring the disciple by configuring him to his Master. Forgiveness is a high point of Christian prayer. Only hearts attuned to God's compassion can receive the gift of prayer. Forgiveness also bears witness that, in our world, love is stronger than sin. Forgiveness is the fundamental condition of the reconciliation of the children of God with their Father and of people with one another.

Legitimate Defense

The legitimate defense of persons and societies is not an exception to the prohibition against the murder of the innocent that constitutes intentional killing. The act of self-defense can have a double effect: the preservation of one's own life and the killing of the aggressor. The one is intended; the other is not (St. Thomas Aquinas, *S Th. II-II, 64, corp. art.*).

An effect can be tolerated without being willed by its agent; for instance, a mother's exhaustion from tending her sick child. A bad effect is not imputable if it was not willed either as an end or as a means of an action, e.g., a death a person incurred in aiding someone in danger. For a bad effect to be imputable, it must be foreseeable, and the agent must have the possibility of avoiding it, as in the case of manslaughter caused by a drunken driver.

Love toward oneself remains a fundamental principle of morality. Therefore, it is legitimate to insist on respect for one's own right to life. Someone who defends his or her life is not guilty of murder, even if he or she is forced to deal his or her aggressor a lethal blow.

Legitimate defense can be not only a right but also a grave duty for someone responsible for another's life, the common good of the family, or the good of the state. Submission to authority and co-responsibility for the common good make it morally obligatory to defend one's country. Preserving the common good of society requires rendering the aggressor unable to inflict harm. For this reason, the traditional teaching of the Church has acknowledged as well-founded the right and duty of legitimate public authority to punish malefactors by means of penalties commensurate with the gravity of the crime, not excluding, in cases of extreme gravity, the death penalty. For analogous reasons, those holding authority have the right to repel by armed force aggressors against the community in their charge.

"Human society can be neither well-ordered nor prosperous unless it has some people invested with legitimate authority to preserve its institutions and to devote themselves, as far as is necessary, to work and care for the good of all" (Pope John XXIII).

By "authority" one means the quality by virtue of which persons or institutions make laws and give orders to people and expect obedience from them. Every human community needs an authority to govern it. The foundation of such authority lies in human nature. It is necessary for the unity of the state. Its role is to ensure, as far as possible, the common good of the society.

If bloodless means are sufficient to defend human lives against an aggressor and to protect public order and the safety of persons, public authority should limit itself to such means because they better correspond to the concrete conditions of the common good and are more in conformity to the dignity of the human person.

Intentional Homicide

The fifth commandment forbids *direct and*

intentional killing as gravely sinful. The murderer and those who cooperate voluntarily in murder commit a sin that cries out to heaven for vengeance. Infanticide, fratricide, patricide, and the murder of a spouse are especially grave crimes by reason of the natural bonds that they break. Concern for eugenics or public health cannot justify any murder, even if commanded by public authority.

The fifth commandment forbids doing anything with the intention of *indirectly* bringing about a person's death. The moral law prohibits exposing someone to mortal danger without grave reason as well as refusing assistance to a person in danger. The acceptance by human society of murderous famines, without efforts to remedy them, is a scandalous injustice and a grave offense. Those whose usurious and avaricious dealings lead to the hunger and death of their brethren in the human family indirectly commit homicide, which is imputable to them (cf. Amos 8-4-10).

Unintentional killing is not morally imputable, but one is not exonerated from grave offense if, without proportionate reasons, he or she has acted in a way that brings about someone's death, even without the intention to do so. The virtue of temperance disposes us to *avoid every kind of excess*: the abuse of food, alcohol, tobacco, or medicine. Those incur grave guilt who, by drunkenness or a love of speed, endanger their own and others' safety on the road, at sea, or in the air.

Temperance is the moral virtue that moderates the attraction of pleasures and provides balance in the use of created goods. It ensures the will's mastery over instincts and keeps desires within the limits of what is honorable. The temperate person directs the sensitive appetites toward what is good and maintains a healthy discretion.

Abortion

Human life must be respected and protected absolutely from the moment of conception. From the first moment of his or her existence, a human being must be recognized as having the rights of a person, among which is the inviolable right of every innocent being to life (*The Gift of Life I, I*).

Endowed with a spiritual and immortal soul, the human person is the only person on earth that God has willed for its own sake. From his or her conception, he or she is destined for eternal beatitude. "Before I formed you in the womb, I knew you; and before you were born, I dedicated you" (Jeremiah 1:5; cf. Job 10:8-12; Psalm 22:10 & 11). "My soul, also, you knew full well, nor was my frame unknown to you when I was fashioned in the depths of the earth" (Psalm 139:14 b & 15).

Since the first century, the Church has affirmed the moral evil of every procured abortion. This teaching has not changed and remains unchangeable. Direct abortion, that is to say, abortion willed either as an end or a means, is gravely contrary to the moral law: "You shall not kill the embryo by abortion and shall not cause the newborn to perish" (*Didache 2, 2*).

"For us, murder is once and for all forbidden. Even the child in the womb, while yet the mother's blood is still being drawn on to form the human being, it is not lawful for us to destroy. To forbid birth is only to murder the sooner. It makes no difference whether one takes away the life once born or destroys it as it comes to birth. He is a person who is to be a person; the fruit is always present in the seed" (Tertullian c 220, *Apology 9:8*).

"A woman who deliberately destroys a fetus is answerable for murder. And any fine distinction as to its being completely formed or unformed is not admissible among us" (St. Basil the Great, *Letter 188*).

God, the author of life, has entrusted to human beings the noble mission of safeguarding life, and people must carry it out in a manner worthy of themselves. Life must be protected with the utmost care from the moment of conception: abortion and infanticide are abominable crimes. Formal cooperation in an abortion constitutes a grave offense.

The Church attaches the canonical penalty of excommunication to this crime against human life. The Church does not, thereby, intend to restrict the scope of mercy. Rather, she makes clear the gravity of the crime committed, the irreparable harm done to the innocent who is put to death as well as to the parents and the whole society.

The inalienable right to life of every innocent human individual is a *constitutive element of a civil society and its legislation.* "The inalienable rights of the person must be recognized and respected by civil society and the political authority. These human rights depend neither on single individuals nor on parents, nor do they represent a concession made by society and the state. They belong to human nature and are inherent in a person by virtue of the creative act from which the person took his or her origin. Among such fundamental rights, one should mention, in this regard, every human being's right to life and physical integrity from the moment of conception until death.

"The moment a positive law deprives a category of human beings of the protection which civil legislation ought to accord them, the state is denying the equality of all before the law. When the state does not place its power at the service of the rights of each citizen, and, in particular, of the more vulnerable, the very foundations of a state based on law are undermined. As a consequence of the protection and respect that must be ensured for the unborn child from the moment of conception, the law must provide appropriate penal sanctions for every deliberate violation of the child's rights" (*The Gift of Life III*).

Since it must be treated from conception as a person, the embryo must be defended in its integrity, cared for, and healed, as far as possible, like any other human being.

"*Prenatal diagnosis* is morally licit 'if it respects the life and integrity of the embryo and the human fetus and is directed toward its safeguarding or healing as an individual. It is gravely opposed to the moral law when this is done with the thought of possibly inducing an abortion, depending upon the results: a diagnosis must not be the equivalent of a death sentence'" (*The Gift of Life I, 2*).

"One must hold as licit procedures carried out on the human embryo that respect the life and integrity of the embryo, do not involve disproportionate risk for it, and are directed toward its healing, the improvement of its condition of health, or its individual survival" (*The Gift of Life I, 3*).

"It is immoral to produce human embryos intended for exploitation as disposable biological material" (*The Gift of Life I, 5*).

"Certain attempts to *influence chromosomal or genetic inheritance* are not therapeutic but are aimed at producing human beings selected according to sex or other predetermined qualities. Such manipulations are contrary to the personal dignity of the human being and his or her integrity and identity, which are unique and unrepeatable" *The Gift of Life I, 6*).

Euthanasia or "Mercy Killing"

Those whose lives are diminished or weakened deserve special respect. Sick or handicapped persons should be helped to lead lives as normal as possible. Christ's compassion toward the sick and his many healings of every kind of infirmity are a resplendent sign that "God has visited his people" (Luke 7:16; cf. Matthew 4:24) and that the kingdom of God is close at hand.

Jesus has the power not only to heal but also to forgive sins (cf. Mark 2:5-12). He has come to heal the whole person, soul and body. He is the physician the sick have need of (cf. Mark 2:17). His compassion toward all who suffer goes so far that he identifies himself with them: "I was ill, and you cared for me" (Matthew 25:36). His preferential love for the sick has not ceased through the centuries to draw the very special attention of Christians toward all those who suffer in body and soul. It is the source of tireless efforts to comfort them.

Whatever its motives and means, direct euthanasia consists in putting an end to the lives of handicapped, sick, or dying persons. It is morally unacceptable. Thus, an act or omission which, of itself or by intention, causes death in order to eliminate suffering constitutes a murder gravely contrary to the dignity of the human person and to the respect due to the living God, his or her Creator. The error of judgment into which one can fall in good faith does not change the nature of this murderous act, which must always be forbidden and excluded.

Discontinuing medical procedures that are burdensome, dangerous, extraordinary, or disproportionate to the expected outcome can be legitimate; it is the refusal of "over-zealous" treatment. Here, one does not will to cause death; one's inability to impede it is merely accepted. The decisions should be made by the patient if he or she is competent and able or, if not, by those legally entitled to act for the patient, whose reasonable will and legitimate interests must be always respected.

Even if death is thought imminent, the ordinary care owed to a sick person cannot be legitimately interrupted. The use of painkillers to alleviate the sufferings of the dying, even at the risk of shortening their days, can be morally in conformity with human dignity if death is not willed as either an end or a means but only foreseen and tolerated as inevitable. Palliative care is a special form of disinterested charity. As such, it should be encouraged.

Suicide

Everyone is responsible for his or her life before God, who has given it. It is God who remains the sovereign Master of life. We are obliged to accept life gratefully and preserve it for his honor and the salvation of our souls. We are stewards, not owners, of the life God has entrusted to us. It is not ours to dispose of.

Suicide contradicts the natural inclination of the human being to preserve and perpetuate his or her life. It is gravely contrary to the just love of self. It likewise offends love of neighbor because it unjustly breaks the ties of solidarity with family, nation, and other human societies to which we continue to have obligations. Suicide is contrary to love for the living God.

The fourth commandment *illuminates other relationships in society*. In our brothers and sisters, we see the children of our parents, in our cousins, the descendents of our ancestors, in our fellow citizens, the children of our country, in the baptized, the children of our mother, the Church, in every human person, a son or daughter of the One who wants to be called "our Father." In this way, our relationships with our neighbors are recognized as personal in character.

The neighbor is not a "unit" in the human collective. He or she is "someone" who, by his or her known origins, deserves particular attention and respect.

If suicide is committed with the intention of setting an example, especially to the young, it also takes on the gravity of scandal. Scandal is an attitude or behavior that leads another to do evil. Scandal is a grave offense if, by deed or omission, another is deliberately led into a grave offense.

The person who gives scandal becomes his or her neighbor's tempter. He or she damages virtue and integrity and may even draw his or her brother or sister into spiritual death.

Anyone who uses the power at his or her disposal in such a way that it leads others to do wrong becomes guilty of scandal and is responsible for the evil that he or she has directly or indirectly encouraged. Voluntary cooperation in suicide is also contrary to the moral law.

Imputability and responsibility for an action can be diminished or even nullified by ignorance, inadvertence, duress, fear, habit, inordinate attachments, and other psychological or social factors. Grave psychological disturbances, anguish, or grave fear of hardship, suffering, or torture can diminish the responsibility of the one committing suicide. Thus, we should not despair of the eternal salvation of persons who have taken their own lives. By ways know to him or her alone, God can provide the opportunity for salutary repentance. For this reason, the Church prays for persons who have taken their own lives.

--compiled by Patrick J. Hession from *The Catechism of the Catholic Church*

Be Careful How You Sow

This is a word of caution, and, perhaps, a word of wisdom about people that come from other Christian communities, Catholic, Protestant, or other. It is wrong to assume that those communities are not doing Christ's work of reaching and nurturing their members because their people don't seem to know much about God the way we think we do.

Sometimes people don't hear what is being preached or taught. Sometimes people don't want to hear because of what God calls their "hardness of heart." Sometimes their faith is weak, and they are not ready to respond. Some people "Church-hop," not to grow and mature but simply because a friend invites them or entices them with something that sounds "new and exciting." It doesn't seem to matter what church or denomination they hop to. I have found all of these factors to be true in every faith community with which I have been in contact over the years, and they are many.

Then, there is the arrogant self-righteousness of those who assume that their denomination is the only one that has the "truth" and that every other is wrong. I have read many "statements of faith" and have always been amazed at those who say they are "standing on the Word." If this is true, why is there so much division in the Church? Is it not, rather, that they are standing on their own *interpretation* of the Word and that, perhaps, their interpretation is limited or even wrong? Heresy still abounds in the Church today.

There are many more trees in a forest than the ones we see in front of us. If we define all trees by the few we see in our immediate vision, we are probably missing something in our definition. Perhaps we need to take a deeper walk into the forest!

The Church is full of babies. Once in a while, some of them grow up. This may mean going through the painful process of "spiritual adolescence." It took me about 35 years to get through that process, and I had four years of theological training! It wasn't that I wasn't "saved" or didn't have knowledge of God. I still needed to be loved and nurtured in a way that I hadn't been up to that time. This is called discipling and is the responsibility of all members of God's family, not just the pastor.

I was gently loved and nurtured into a personal relationship with God over several months. I was never asked or encouraged to leave the Church to which I belonged. Had I been "preached at" or thrown tracts without a relationship, I would have run the other way as fast as I could!

People who didn't even know me or attempt to know me have tossed tracts at me at work. I had all I could do to keep from tearing them up and throwing them back in their face because they did not do it with love or with any concern about whether I already had a relationship with God. Articles, tracts, and books have their place as seeds. But, they cannot be forced upon people or thrust in their face.

The "word" that gave rise to this chapter is this: "If there is rotten or defective seed in the garden, do we blame the gardener? If a child is born with a defect, do we blame the parents?"

The gardener, of course, is responsible to nurture the seed that he planted, but he doesn't always know the quality of the seed. He trusts that that seed that he planted was good seed.

Parents who give birth to a defective child try to nurture that child as best they can. Sometime it takes a long time for the child to mature; sometimes it never does. The child needs to be loved not criticized and condemned or taken out of that family and brought into another family that one thinks is "better."

Over the years, I have heard people rejoicing about someone being "saved" from the Catholic or some other church. This actually happened to me. This betrays ignorance of other faith communities and doesn't glorify God.

Each babe in Christ needs to be loved and nurtured into a meaningful relationship with God, just as we all need to be nurtured into maturity as a productive member of society. People need to feel and experience God's love in a real way from one of his children who really knows him. That doesn't mean that they have to be taken out of their own faith community. God himself may do so, but he has the right to, we don't.

People are ready to hear about and accept God at different times, maybe a whole lifetime, maybe never. It took my mother-in-law 89 years. Many people, even in the natural, have trouble accepting love because they have never experienced it in any meaningful way before. We need to be very patient with people.

Many factors impact our lives, and they are not all from Satan. Remember the parable of the sower. A pessimistic reading indicates only 1 in 4 makes it. A more positive reading may indicate that we need to do more with the other 3 so they can also make it.

God is a lot more merciful than many of his "servants." Even some of the disciples wanted to call fire down from heaven! Sometimes the ground in which we sow has to be carefully tilled before the seed is sown. We need to remove the rocks not put stumbling blocks or boulders in the way! Sometimes, as Jesus himself said, the rocks or pebbles are in our own eyes! Be sure they are removed from your eyes, then, before you try to remove them from others.

--Patrick J. Hession

Bibliography

Bettenson, Henry, Ed., Documents of the Christian Church, 2nd. Edition, Copyright 1963, Oxford University Press

Cassels, Louis, What's the Difference? A Comparison Of The Faiths Men Live By, Louis Cassels, Copyright 1965, Waymark Books, 1968

Dollen, Msgr. Charles, The Book of Catholic Wisdom, copyright 1986, Our Sunday Visitor Publishing Division

Fuller, Reginald C., D.D., Ph. D., L.S.S., General Editor, A New Catholic Commentary on Sacred Scripturue, Copyright 1969, Catholic Biblical Association, Thomas Nelson, Inc., Publisher

Girzone, Joseph E., Joshua: The Homecoming, copyright 1999, Doubleday, a division of Random House, Inc.

Grodi, Marcus, How Firm a Foundation, copyright 2002, Coming Home Resources, OH

Rahner, Karl, Ed., Encyclopedia of Theology, copyright 1986, The Crossroad Publishing Company. NY

About the Author

In addition to four years of Theological Studies, Patrick holds a Master's Degree with a double major in Counseling Psychology and Social Psychology and a Bachelor's Degree in Philosophy.

After a few years of wandering in the spiritual wilderness, by the mercy and grace of God and through the love and concern of a servant of God, Patrick rediscovered the God Who Is Family, to which he and you are called to belong. Since then, he has continued to experience the healing and restoration that only God can bring. Working as a minister of reconciliation, Patrick calls all people to be and to live as members of the Family Who Is God. Visit www.familytofamilies.com for further information. You can also reach him at familytofamilies@hotmail.com or 336-667-2355.

www.ingramcontent.com/pod-product-compliance
Lightning Source LLC
Chambersburg PA
CBHW020944230426
43666CB00005B/157